CW00868461

That's Life

BY THE SAME AUTHOR

At Sea
True Loves
It Could Be Worse

That's Life

A PERSONAL & HIGHLY PREJUDICED VIEW OF LIFE'S IRRITATIONS

Lester Wertheimer

iUniverse®

That's Life
A PERSONAL & HIGHLY PREJUDICED VIEW OF LIFE'S IRRITATIONS

iUniverse books may be ordered through booksellers or by contacting:

iUniverse
1663 Liberty Drive
Bloomington, IN 47403
www.iuniverse.com
1-800-Authors (1-800-288-4677)

ISBN: 978-1-5320-4371-0 (sc)
ISBN: 978-1-5320-4373-4 (hc)
ISBN: 978-1-5320-4372-7 (e)

Library of Congress Control Number: 2018902370

Print information available on the last page.

iUniverse rev. date: 04/12/2018

Contents

Preface   1

Parenthood   5

Brotherhood   11

Forbidden Subjects   17

Names   23

Pets   29

Cars   35

Art   43

Romance   49

Food   55

Nice vs. Nasty   61

Health   67

Investing   75

Attitude   81

Music   89

Cruelty   97

Humor   105

Weather   113

Sports   119

Lies & Liars   127

Fashion   133

Anger   139

Frank Lloyd Wright   145

Work   151

Travel   157

Fear   163

Friendship   169

Drinking   175

Sex   183

Death   191

Dedicated to the latest generation of
Lewins, Murrays, and Wertheimers
Brilliant kids all–making us proud.

Preface

My wife and I had five children from previous marriages, and those children eventually produced children of their own. So we now have an attractive mixture of eight grandchildren, consisting of four boys and four girls. They are perfect in every way, of course, since their own parents were also products of perfect upbringings.

Becoming a grandparent is largely beyond your control; it is entirely up to your child and his or her spouse, and at best, may be influenced by their childhood experiences. But don't kid yourself; you had little to do with it. If your children choose to remain childless, the grandparent experience will have passed you by, and you might consider buying a puppy instead.

It should be obvious that being a grandparent is considerably different from being a parent. While most parents stumble through the quirks of child care—often unsure if they are doing the right thing—grandparents committed their blunders long ago, making them more certain these days about those difficult decisions and proper courses of action. Whether or not your child accepts grandparental advice, most will at least listen to voices of experience before rejecting them outright.

It also helps to recall one's own experience with grandparents, though in my case those encounters were minimal. The father of my father was conscripted into the Austro-Hungarian army and fought in one of those endless wars around the end of the 19th century. Returning home one evening during a snowstorm he peeked in the window of their house before entering. His children spotted him and cried, "Daddy's home!" They rushed outside and found the collapsed body of the returning warrior, who had just suffered a fatal heart attack. My own father was about six months old at the time and had no recollection of that incident—or of his father. So, of course, neither do I.

My mother's father immigrated to this country with his wife and their six children, including my mother, who was less than a year old. He had been a baker in Kalvaria, Poland, and was married three times; the first two wives having died in childbirth. This prolific man produced a total of twenty-four children among his three wives, and one cannot help wonder when he found time to bake even a single bagel. It also remains a mystery how he remembered the name of every kid. In fact, it was discovered years ago that he actually gave two daughters the very same name.

I remember my grandfather as a gentle man with a long gray beard, always sitting at the kitchen table, reading a foreign newspaper and drinking hot tea from a glass. We never spoke, as he knew no English, but he often patted me softly on the head. He died when I was five and now remains no more than a footnote in my life.

Learning how to be the perfect grandfather, therefore, without actually experiencing one myself, was pretty much a do-it-yourself project. As the closest grandchildren live nearly a three-hour drive away, and the others even a far greater distance, a spontaneous round of charades or even a quick game of Old Maid is not possible. The entire family does gather for a week each summer at a Mexican resort, where shoes are optional, the water is warm, and close relationships are renewed and relished. But the extent of my influence has been little more than that of an absentee critic and advisor, neither of which is totally satisfactory to the grandchildren or to me.

I decided, therefore, that my most valuable legacy would be to write a series of short essays on subjects I consider important in life, for example, Art, Romance, and Humor, in the hope that our grandchildren might benefit from our life experiences. Those who know me realize I have—as the subtitle of this book states—personal and highly prejudiced views on most subjects, especially life's irritations. This might not qualify me to offer foolproof advice for avoiding the potholes of life, but it may serve to make more bearable the inevitable frustrations one will likely face.

The following chapters are personal observations, sentiments, and opinions, developed over several decades that form a legacy intended for the benefit of grandchildren. It is hoped that others, as well, may find them beneficial and perhaps even entertaining.

Parenthood

It probably comes as no surprise that you do not choose your own parents. You are not consulted about this most important of all decisions, nor are you given a choice. It's completely out of your hands, having been decided several months before you are born. At the time of your birth it's already too late. The die has been cast, as they say, and what has been determined cannot be undone. Before you know it, there they are, two total strangers, hovering over your crib, babbling baby sounds and acting like second-rate actors in a third-rate play. Who are these people? Where did they come from? They seem nice enough, but honestly, don't you think it would have been more reasonable to be asked your opinion beforehand?

If you were able to select your own parents you could eliminate those with loud voices, unpleasant behavior, and offensive odors. You would choose parents with agreeable personalities who displayed no visible signs of anxiety or other worrisome behavior. Obviously, you would reject those with a criminal past, problems with alcohol or drugs, and others who exhibit hostility toward children and small animals. You would certainly do better without compulsive types or anyone with an inflated ego. You would also eliminate the uneducated, the insensitive, and every notoriously bad driver, including those who refuse to use their turn indicators. In other words, your parents would be perfect, which I think is the least one deserves.

But none of that is going to happen, because you were never given the option of selecting these people in the first place. So there they are; you're stuck with them—as they are with you—and from the way they act it looks like they're planning to hang around forever. Actually, it isn't all bad. They feed you regularly, wipe your bottom when necessary, and speak softly when you want to sleep. On the other hand, there are endless new rules one is expected to follow and certain procedures that encourage behavior often contrary to one's instincts. If you ask me, the whole arrangement is fraught with complications and could certainly be improved.

Life was much easier before. There I was—as I recall—floating around in that warm, comfortable space. I never felt the pangs of hunger nor did I want for anything. Best of all, my bottom didn't need to be diapered and I didn't have to wear a stupid hat. Everything was so agreeable there was nothing to complain about. And then suddenly, without warning, all hell broke loose! One day, from out of nowhere, my secluded spa sprang a leak. It began as a trickle, and before I knew it, the leak became a torrent and I was swimming for my life. I was being sucked down to that small opening below. The passage was so narrow a sardine would have had trouble getting through it. Holy crap! I thought; how will I ever survive this? I had no way of knowing what I was in for, since the entire experience happened long before I realized my happy existence came with a due date. Silly me, I figured my world was the way it was, and change was not only improbable, but completely out of the question.

With every contraction pushing me lower I heard a woman's voice groaning and cursing. She was making a terrific scene—yelling her head off and using several four-letter words I'd never heard before. The unpleasantness was mostly directed at someone who was either hard of hearing or frightened to death, because he never uttered a word. She was saying how all this was *his* fault. I mean, really, who needed to hear all that?

Finally my head reached the end of the long channel and I came up against a brick wall. But it wasn't actually brick, because it began to expand. After a considerable, and mostly anxious time for me, it opened wider, and with a terrific effort my head began to emerge. Now I could clearly hear the conversations, the shrieks, and several voices yelling, "Push! Dammit, push!" I hoped they weren't talking to me, because I was doing my best but still having an awful time understanding what the hell was going on.

Then suddenly it was over, and I winced in pain from the blast of cold air and the blinding light. As if that weren't bad enough, some officious guy in a white gown was sucking fluid out of my nose and mouth, after which I took my first breath. The air tasted funny, but breathing for myself was oddly exhilarating. The guy in the white gown then snipped off the cord coming out of my stomach. It didn't really hurt, but I began to cry anyway. Who the hell did he think he was, treating me like that? Then his assistants took over—compulsively wiping, washing, weighing, measuring, and generally eliminating the last shred of dignity that remained. They checked my heart rate, respiration, muscle tone, and reflex reactions until I wanted to yell, "Enough already! You've had your fun, now get lost!" I'd never been so manhandled or felt so irritated. I wasn't even fifteen minutes old and this had become not only the first, but also the worst day of my life.

Eventually, I was taken to my mother, who I discovered was the person doing the screaming, swearing, and carrying on just moments before. They laid me on her stomach and she began to feed me from her breast. I have to say, it was the only good thing that happened to me since the whole circus began, and in no time I was asleep.

When I awoke, I was no longer nude. I had on a truly hideous outfit, complete with silly hat that looked like something from a Halloween party for the mentally challenged. It was blue, of course, and decorated with little monkeys swinging from trees. The hat also had a monkey holding onto a branch with one hand and a banana in the other. I mean really, whose incredibly bad taste was behind all that?

Unfortunately, the annoyances kept coming like series of tropical storms. Before leaving the hospital I heard talk of something called "circumcision." I didn't quite understand what that was all about, but recent experience—and a hint that this might actually involved my weenie—made me anxious. How dare anyone touch my private parts! This was pretty much the last straw! But before I could do anything about it the deed was done, and there I was, with wounds to my pride as well as my favorite toy.

That's Life

I've got to say, being born was just the start of regular irritations and endless frustration. Nobody likes change, and even a fetus—one that appreciates consistency as much as the next guy—considers any change annoying, regardless of the reason. Getting accustomed to this new existence was challenging; I mean there were serious adjustments involved. If I wanted anything I practically had to cry my lungs out. I never had to do that before I was born. Now it seemed I was always crying. And my parents acted as if they had no idea what I was crying about. I realize this wasn't an everyday event, but really, how could they be surprised by every little squawk?

"What does my darling little Peter want?" asked my mother. Now that's another thing; who dreamed up that name? And why wasn't I consulted? Months earlier, I thought my name should be Hieronymus. I have no idea where that came from, but I liked the sound of it. Hieronymus had a nice ring to it, a bit regal I thought, a hint of history and on the barely acceptable side of pretention.

"What do you want," she asked? "What do you think I want?" were the words in my head. "It doesn't take a Masters Degree in Sociology to realize I'm hungry and my bed is wet, for crying out loud!"

"If only you could speak," she would say.

"I am speaking," I would answer. "You just don't understand the sounds I'm making". So there we were, as frustrated as any ancient character at the Tower of Babel. I must say this early period was one endless pain in the neck after another.

It was a few uncomfortable months before things began to change. After a while I was able to make a few sounds my parents seemed to understand. They were actually the very same words I had been speaking in my head since being born, but finally, they were being understood. Thank God I didn't give up on those two, even though I was ready to throw in the towel months earlier.

It became even easier just prior to celebrating the first anniversary of my arrival. That's when I took my first steps. The slow and uncomfortable crawling days were over, my sore knees began to heal, and I couldn't have been happier about my physical progress. Once I discovered the thrill of full-speed self-locomotion I hardly ever slowed down. In fact, for a while they had me on a leash. Honest to God, a leash! Whenever we left the house for a walk I was tethered like a goddam puppy. It was not only humiliating but people looked at me like I was some kind of freakish combination of toddler and terrier.

Each day brought new experiences and discoveries. The most astounding of these occurred a week or two after being born. I sensed another person was sharing my new world. I was aware of him earlier, but he had remained cool and distant and we'd never been formally introduced. One day he approached with some hesitation, and my mother said, "This is your brother, Alan. Can you say, Hello, Alan?" Seriously? At two weeks of age she wanted me to say, "Hello, Alan?" Even if I could, I didn't want to. I figured there were already too many people in my life. I hadn't quite abandoned the fantasy of returning to those wonderful pre-birth days, those delightful solitary moments when I was happily alone in my private spa and not overwhelmed by attention.

A few days later, the little kid called Alan came over and gave me a loving hug that nearly cracked a couple of ribs. My screams scared him away, and I didn't see him again for a week. It was not yet the fraternal relationship our parents envisioned, and if it were up to me, it probably never would be.

With all my complaints, the shock of being born and the unwelcome changes in my life, you might get the idea that it was a horrible introduction to "life on the outside", as I thought of it. Well, it was bad enough to put me in a sour mood for the first few months, but eventually I came to realize these parents were pretty nice people. Granted, it took a while to sink in, but I eventually discovered they were relatively good folks, and compared to others passing through, I was pretty lucky.

I didn't feel exactly the same about that Alan fellow. He and I remained suspicious of one another for years, and the thaw didn't come until we were practically adults. In retrospect that was a damn shame. They say you can choose your friends but not your relatives. There's a lot of truth in that—and take it from me—it's another damn shame. But I suppose that's life, and there's not a whole lot you can do about it.

Brotherhood

In the Broadway show "How to Succeed in Business" there's a song about brotherhood:

There is a brotherhood of man
A benevolent brotherhood of man
A noble tie that binds all human hearts and minds
Into one big brotherhood of man

Brotherhood! What a beautiful thought, one to which we all aspire, but sadly, often fall short. In fact, brotherhood was light-years away from what I experienced. The little kid called Alan and I never even learned to spell the word. We seemed so different from one another I strongly suspected we had different parents. I imagined my real parents abandoned me on the doorstep, and I was taken in and raised by others, because they were basically good and decent people. My brother was quick to reinforce the notion that I was illegitimate.

"They bought you at the five-and-dime store," he declared, "and since nobody else wanted you, they got you for about a nickel. I personally think they overpaid."

My parents made every attempt to bring us closer, but the ideal fraternal relationship was a fantasy that never stood a chance. Since Alan had experienced the undivided love and attention of his parents for his first two years, he strongly resented the intrusion of a stranger in his life. He considered me a hostile alien from an evil planet who fell to earth with the sole purpose of disrupting his perfect world. He was jealous, competitive, and supremely antagonistic. Psychiatrists call that sibling rivalry. Alan considered it betrayal, and I thought–no matter what you call it–it was a miserable way to grow up.

"Why don't we send him back where he came from?" asked my desperate brother. "He doesn't seem happy here; I mean he's always crying. Maybe we can sell him. Yeah, there's an idea; we can sell him and get a puppy instead."

"We are not getting rid of the baby," said my mother. "He's part of the family, and we're all going to get along." Unfortunately, our parents were the only ones who embraced that idea; the brothers were having none of it. We genuinely disliked one another, and learning to get along was like learning to love my mother's invariably overcooked string beans.

Alan was nearly two years older than I. He was taller, physically stronger, and consistently dumber. He preferred baseball to basic math and rabble-rousing to reading. As the most ordinary of ordinary students he firmly believed one's greatest aspiration should be to pass on to the next higher grade without actually doing homework. His saving graces were his good looks and charming personality. He was, essentially, a movie-star-handsome con man.

During our earliest years we lived in apartments that never had more than two bedrooms. This meant that Alan and I always shared a room, an arrangement we both resented. I considered it similar to having a cellmate you could never turn your back on, if you knew what was good for you. Being older, bigger, and stronger Alan assumed he was entitled to a larger portion of our space. The concept of sharing equally, if it ever crossed his mind, was dismissed faster than the speed of light. Many of our fights were similar to border disputes between belligerent nations. Though I attempted to establish reasonable rules, Alan's lack of fair play ran roughshod over every one of them.

Complaints to our parents resulted in their assessment that Alan was antagonistic and I was intolerant. In other words we shared the blame equally. I continued to wonder how I was supposed to tolerate unwarranted attacks from an irrational bully. I now realize that I probably irritated Alan nearly as much as he annoyed me. My strict sense of neatness and order conflicted with his brutish ways that closely resembled those of Attila the Hun. When I first called him that he had no idea who that was, but he suspected it was derogatory.

"Not particularly," I stated. "You should be flattered. Attila not only needed to succeed, but wasn't satisfied until everyone else failed. Kind of reflects your philosophy, wouldn't you say?" For several months Alan remained unsure if being compared to a Hun was a complement or an insult.

In many ways Alan was like an unruly family pet; one who refuses to be housebroken, barks at passing puppies, and nips at visitors' ankles. Though regularly petted, fed, and bathed, he invariably created more aggravation than pleasure. I, for one, would have had little regret returning him to the pound. The more practical solution, however, was to go our individual ways, have separate friends, unrelated interests, and lead uniquely different lives. Our relationship continued that way for most of our early years.

After what seemed an eternity, Alan shocked us all and graduated from high school. He decided to join the Army Air Corps, rather than wait to be drafted into the Army. This event was an important adjustment for our family, most significantly, me. Finally, the thorn in my side, my perpetual migraine, and the major irritant in my life would be leaving the nest. It was ostensibly to fight Nazis and Japs, but I assumed it was more likely that his presence would disrupt the War Department, or perhaps challenge the U.S. Constitution itself.

On the morning he left for the Induction Center it suddenly struck me that I may never see my brother again. Wars are notoriously dangerous, and as everyone knows, many warriors don't survive. As I shook Alan's hand a lump got stuck in my throat. I was rarely at a loss for words, but on this occasion I hardly knew what to say to my lifelong enemy number one. After an embarrassing pause I said, "Take care of yourself, big guy, and stay out of trouble."

"I had no idea you cared," he replied.

"Well actually I don't, but if anything goes wrong it would upset our parents."

"You lying bastard—I know you really care."

And with that he wrapped his arms around me and gave me a bear hug that would have fractured the ribs of a genuine grizzly. He also gave me the keys to his 1936 Ford convertible. "Take care of my car, you little *putz*, and remember it's mine, not yours. If I see the slightest ding on any body part, when I get back, I'll do the same to every one of your body parts."

And then he was gone for two years, which made me deliriously happy. Every so often, however, I missed having him around. Sounds silly, I know, but I suppose he had become a bad habit–like marijuana or martinis–and to some degree I was hooked.

When Alan returned to civilian life, I was already in college. His two years, mostly spent at an Air Force base in Utah, had virtually no effect on his maturity or irritating personality. I thought, what a damn shame; he's still a jerk. He enrolled at a business school to study accounting, while I continued pursuit of an architectural education. Upon the constant urging of our parents I invited Alan to spend a football weekend with me. It was the Cal–Stanford annual game, and I continued to fear that Alan would find some way to embarrass me. As it turned out I was mistaken. Alan was the perfect guest who entertained us all with dramatic stories of fearless antics on leave and endless sexual conquests throughout the state of Utah.

"Tell me, Alan," I asked later, "were any of those stories true?"

"What difference does it make? Your friends loved them."

A few months later Alan became engaged. It was a surprise to many of us who believed his enviable bachelor life rivaled that of a Hollywood leading man. Since puberty he had been desired by women of all ages, many of them great beauties, but sadly, none of them Phi Beta Kappa material. During the war years, while a senior in high school, Alan worked the swing shift at Douglas Aircraft in Santa Monica. As most young men at that time were in the service Alan was in great demand as a desirable sexual object. It was a role he was born to play, and he did so with dedication and gusto.

So who could his fiancée be? As it turned out she was the only daughter of a successful businessman. She was not nearly as stunning as many of those he formerly dated, but she was cheerful, pleasant, and not least of all, wealthy.

Brotherhood

The wedding took place at the elegant Beverly Hills Hotel, and I attended in the supporting role of "Best Man". I was puzzled when asked to play that part, but felt there was no way to refuse. I gave a wonderful speech that night, if I do say so myself, having been fortified by an endless flow of French champagne. The enthusiastic appreciation by the hundreds in attendance was overwhelming, but of course most were drunk as skunks.

With a quickly growing family and steady job at his father-in-law's manufacturing company Alan quickly became domesticated and—who would have guessed—responsible. Somewhat later, as our offices were close by, we began to have lunch every so often. What I discovered was that there was considerably more substance to Alan than I ever dreamed, or that he had ever revealed. One day after lunch he said, "Come with me; I have to buy a new pair of shoes, and I'm going to buy you a pair, too. Those scruffy things on your feet are an embarrassment." For the first time in my life I felt a sense of brotherhood—honest to God—a genuine feeling of humanity and compassion from my big brother.

A year or two later, Alan bought out his father-in-law's interest in the company and proceeded to grow the business. His previous aggression, charm, and good looks resulted in a steady and considerable success. When he moved to a new office, he insisted I design the space and select the furnishings. It was a dream job for me, and we both celebrated the event with an inaugural party that lasted long into the night.

Later in life we spent a long weekend at a log cabin I had designed and built near Lake Tahoe. It was just the two of us alone, sharing a space for the first time since we were children. We sat on rocking chairs on the porch surrounded by fragrant pine trees, talking about our long dead parents, our families, and life in general.

"You know, you were the bane of my early life," I said. "A real pain in the ass."

"You weren't exactly my cup of tea either," he answered.

"Have you forgiven me for muscling in on your territory?" I asked.

"You know I had nothing to do with that. I never asked to be born."

"Yeah, I forgave you years ago. And now, considering what you've become, I'm proud of you. It's not easy to admit, but I'm actually in awe of you."

I was vacationing at the same cabin two years later when my brother's wife called. "Your brother had an accident," she said. "He was driving to his club for a round of golf when he had a heart attack."

"How is he?" I asked.

"He's dead," she said.

It took a few seconds for the message to penetrate. Then I dropped the phone and burst into tears. It was the only time in my life I had felt such overwhelming grief. I didn't cry when each parent passed away; somehow I knew it was coming. But with my only brother it was an utterly devastating shock.

Mark Twain said, *"The universal brotherhood of man is our most precious possession."* It took nearly a lifetime for me to find the truth in those words.

Forbidden Subjects

It is inevitable that at times you will find yourself in mixed company; that is, among people you barely know or some you've just met for the first time. When that happens, you should be aware that several sensitive subjects must be avoided if you hope to survive the experience. Among these forbidden subjects are politics, religion, sex, and to a certain degree, money. Nearly everyone holds strong feelings about these matters, and some views may not coincide with yours. If, for example, it turns out that most people in the room voted for the Republican candidate, it would be unwise to express your profound regret that the Democratic candidate lost the election and that the winning candidate is a hopeless moron. That sort of thing only leads to ill will, no minds will be changed, and one or more of you will go home frustrated, aggravated, and possibly, with a throbbing migraine.

We all tend to gravitate towards those who hold views similar to ours. Thus, if you are confronted by someone sporting a six-shooter on each hip, who believes those speaking with an accent should go back where they came from, and is convinced the wrong side won the Civil War, well, these are radical attitudes with which you may not agree. So what should you do? If you are prudent you will say nothing, smile politely as you walk away, and silently hope the pathetic extremist walks into an open manhole.

In recent years the two major political parties have become more negative than ever. Majorities in both parties express not just unfavorable views, but genuinely hostile feelings toward each other. Both say the other party is wrongheaded, irrational, and reckless, which has resulted in the two parties becoming polarized to the extent that one side of the aisle barely speaks to the other side. Thus, the business of government has pretty much ground to a halt, and almost nothing gets done. One side blames the other, and both sides refuse to compromise their rigid positions. The electorate has become disgusted with both sides, and many see no point in voting for either side. So much for our esteemed democratic process.

It would help if both parties realized there is no absolute right or wrong. Political issues are ideally settled by compromise in which each side respects the strong feelings of the other, and both sides move closer together. In other words, the resulting agreement will be neither black nor white, but rather an unpopular shade of gray. It is said that a good compromise leaves both sides equally unhappy.

Our country has survived for years under several administrations with a variety of ideas of how governments should govern. Many believe that the less the federal government does the better things will be. In other words, the government should do whatever it takes to keep us safe, but otherwise stay out of our lives. Others believe it is the business of government to help those who are unable to help themselves, and that often takes federal tax money to feed, shelter, and make life more bearable for others. Arguing your views with those who disagree, however, is no more productive than going on a snipe hunt. Why not save your breath, stay home, and bang your head against the wall?

Similar advice applies to religious discussions. Religions are belief systems in which one worships an invisible supernatural power. In other words, there is a God, or call it what you will, "up there" to whom you can turn for spiritual guidance when personal problems become overwhelming and your life is heading toward the dumpster.

Some consider God the most powerful force in their lives, an authority that is held responsible for all manners of behavior. For example, you may have noticed that when a sports figure hits a home run or makes a three-point basket he will look and point skyward to give thanks to an invisible power he believes responsible for the score. On the other hand, when that same person strikes out or misses the shot you will never see him looking upward and shaking his fist in exasperation.

Some might consider these conflicting attitudes hypocritical, and some might be right.

Most people tolerate other religions, even though they may believe some are a bit wacky, because freedom of religious belief is a fundamental principle of our nation. So if someone wants to worship the sun, for example, who are we to say he must be off his rocker? Actually, worshipping the sun is more logical than worshiping other entities, because all of life depends on the sun. Worshipping a totem pole—which is actually a decorated chunk of tree—can be risky, but sunshine offers light, heat, and vegetation, including much of what we eat.

There are over four thousand different faiths in the world today, and though they vary considerably, their principal purpose is to comfort and give direction to our lives. All belief systems began by providing answers to unanswerable questions. For example, why does the sun disappear at night, what is thunder and lightning, and how is it that, after a certain number of years, people keel over and die? The earliest humans assumed there must be some mysterious power controlling those things.

The preoccupation with death goes back as far as the Neanderthals, whose fear of death led them to rationalize death as the beginning of a new cycle, not necessarily the end of life. One of the strongest instincts of mankind is the will to survive and live forever. Even suicide bombers ignore the fear of death by believing they are headed for immortality—one that includes sex with multiple virgins. Good luck with that. To believe there exists a happy hunting ground makes death less frightening and more acceptable.

Every religion claims to be the true religion, and sadly, there's a certain lack of tolerance among them. Some have been at each other's throats for hundreds of years; and in fact, the number of deaths generated in the name of God probably exceeds all other causes. As a result, the commendable policy of "Love Thy Neighbor" remains an unfulfilled fantasy, as it has for centuries.

Religious leaders realized from the start they were selling more than spiritual guidance. By exploiting the fear of death, they sold the promise of eternal life, guided by the concepts of reward and punishment. The cost to enter a heavenly paradise was to blindly follow the church's dictates. The rebellious few who didn't buy that message were told they would wind up in a fiery place of damnation called "hell". Thus, heaven became the reward and hell, the punishment.

What about those with no religion? These days many consider any deity a clever invention meant to explain the unexplainable, while scaring to death those who dare question the very concept. The growing numbers of people who consider themselves agnostics or atheists reject what they believe to be the hypocrisy of organized religion. Most beliefs preach love, acceptance, and a live-and-let-live philosophy, but many don't come within light-years of those ideals. They often reject pre-marital sex, divorce, abortion, and even an occasional puff of marijuana; and many consider homosexuality perverted and immoral.

Worse yet is Sharia Law, a religious legal system that embodies the fundamental concepts of the Islamic faith. Sharia is all-pervasive, in that it regulates public and private behavior and beliefs. For example, criticizing any part of the Quran–the Islamic bible–is punishable by death. Seriously, death!

Most people fail to realize that the Quran, as well as every bible of every religion that has ever existed, was actually written by human beings. It may be presented as the words of a God, but multiple religious authors actually inscribed those words–often reconstructing historical facts long after the events occurred. So putting to death any critic of the Quran seems as vindictive as the idea of to putting Ernest Hemingway in jail because, in your view, the conclusion of "The Old Man and the Sea" was just too depressing for words.

Being homosexual is another way Muslims can be punished; some, in fact, have actually been hung, stoned, or beheaded. It's no joke; being a gay Muslim is as dangerous as walking hatless during a summer hike across Death Valley in flip-flops. Whereas we attempt to separate church and state, Islam combines the two, producing a severe and undeviating legal system. Even stealing, considered a minor crime, may be punished by having your hand chopped off. Ruthless? Absolutely! But as a consequence, theft and burglary in some Islamic countries is as rare as a one-handed person.

In some Islamic nations Sharia law is especially unfriendly to women. For example, females are not permitted to drive a car, husbands may beat their wives for insubordination, and if a wife wants a divorce she needs her husband's permission. Having an extra-marital affair may be punishable by stoning the woman, while the male usually remains free of punishment. Having to wear a veil and full-length black burka in 110-degree weather is a minor irritation by comparison. If you happen to run into an Islamic person at some gathering you might discuss the ruthlessness of Sharia law, but not before planning your escape route.

Churches were once the chief source of education, culture, and political authority. Even a hundred years ago most attended church every single week of the year. You didn't dare miss church unless you had a fever of 102 or a crippling hangover. There was no sleeping in; church attendance was the barometer of your spiritual health.

These days church attendance continues to slide. It is estimated that perhaps no more than 20 percent of the population consider themselves regular churchgoers. And the reasons are many; for example, social conventions have changed and the guilt of not attending church has lessened. Sunday morning, once an entertainment desert, has been replaced by sports on TV, shopping, or simply a day of rest. Finally, regardless of how you feel about religion in general, my original warning remains in effect–discussing any of this in mixed company is playing with fire.

Sex is another subject one should avoid when in the company of people you don't know well. The reasons should be obvious. First of all, sex is extremely personal and no one else's business. In addition, you never know when you're going to run into someone with 19th Century views, such as the notion that babies are delivered by storks. So why embarrass that person with actual facts?

It may be arguable, but some believe when it comes to sex, women talk too much about it with one another, and men often lie about it among themselves. Your attitude might be otherwise, but I think we can all agree it's not necessary to divulge every detail about what happened last Saturday night. Some may talk in great detail to friends, but those are in the minority. Most men I know are gentlemen who rarely kiss and tell, mostly because that's the proper way to act. More importantly, what happens between two people is truly private, as it should be.

People who speak of sexual exploits are often like politicians, who readily throw truth under the bus for a better story. "Dozens of partners, you claim? Really? With your looks and personality a potential partner would have to be blind, sex-starved, and nuttier than a fruitcake to jump in bed with you. That's just a personal opinion, of course."

Trust me on this one; nobody wants to hear your sexual history. No one. If your experience is consistently unsuccessful you're considered pathetic, and if all goes well, no one is likely to believe you. So forget sexual stories and find a different subject. Maybe tell a joke.

The last of the sensitive subjects to avoid in mixed company is anything to do with money. Some people consider money even more private than sex, and pursuit of that subject will not attract many admirers. If you are successful in life you will be respected and disliked at the same time. Having heaps of money makes people envious, and what we envy is often the target of hostility.

One should also avoid prying into others people's financial dealings, chiefly because it's none of your business. Additionally, some people exaggerate what they earn, the amount they pay for things, their success with investments, and the many ways in which they screw the IRS. So monetary facts and figures bandied about in mixed company should be taken with a grain or two of salt.

There are some who insist on knowing what you paid for things, like your new car, lawn mower, or tooth extraction. These are people with little respect for your privacy and even less embarrassment for their intrusiveness. Maybe they're conducting a survey, or curious to know if they overpaid for the same item, but my personal view is that they are simply nosy. Your best response to them might be, "I really have no recollection; but after all, it's only money."

When you are among people you barely know, and any of these situations arise, why not change the subject and discuss the weather? I can assure you—wherever you are—the current weather is unusual. Who could possibly argue about that?

Names

In Shakespeare's Romeo and Juliet the heroine asks,

"What's in a name?
That which we call a rose
By any other name would smell as sweet."

Juliet, a Capulet, was explaining that even though Romeo came from the rival house of Montague, he was still the one she loved. The importance to her was the person, not what the person was called. That also goes for the rest of us. A Sam, an Amanda, or any old Jack can be bright or stupid, thin or fat, generous as Bill Gates or as miserly as Ebenezer Scrooge; the name gives us no clue. On the other hand, certain names have particular connotations. We would expect a girl named "Merry" to have a lovely disposition, while a boy named "Adolph" has not been spotted since the annihilation of the Third Reich in 1944.

Nobody really knows how naming people and things got started, but we can guess the practice has been around since the beginning of civilization. The purpose of naming was to identify and distinguish one person or thing from another. If, for example, every Neanderthal were named Zog and someone yelled, "Hey, Zog, got a minute?" every tribal member would stop what he was doing and reply, "Who, me?" So individuals were assigned a unique name that would distinguish one from another. Thus, there would be, for example, only one Zog, one Ugg, and one Grok in each tribe. Years later, as civilization developed, groups formed families, and there was a need to identify those sharing a cave, tent, or palace. This led to the development of a surname, a last name shared by close members of the same group, like the Capulets, Medicis, or Kardashians.

An interesting story involves a fellow architect I once knew, Aaron Rosenzweig. Aaron fell crazy in love with a bright and attractive woman named Erin. You can see where this is going. Every so often someone might say, "Tell me, Aaron/Erin, how do you feel about...?" And, of course, no one knew to whom the speaker was referring. Neither Aaron nor Erin wanted to force the other to change his or her name, so they decided to change both names. They agreed that with a handle like "Rosenzweig" a one-syllable name would be preferable. They also wanted to maintain the first letter of their original names, because their wedding gifts included countless monogrammed linens. Thus, Aaron became Art Rozsenzweig and Erin became Eve. Their new names confused most of their friends, not to mention perplexed family members, but over time everyone overcame that obstacle, and the Rosenzweigs lived their life happily ever after.

The naming of persons and things throughout history was often arbitrary. For example, we call a certain writing instrument a pencil, though it just as easily might have been called a horse, if that name weren't already used to describe a four-footed animal. Names were often developed from a person's appearance (Longfellow), personal trait (Prudence), occupation (Miller), location (Madison), or sometimes from nature (Daisy, or Rose). The popularity of names has always been transitory. Two hundred years ago the most popular baby names were Mary and John, whereas today those names are Emma and Noah. Popular baby names next year will probably be something else.

It has been established through extensive psychological research that certain names are considered more desirable than others. For example, David, Diane, Jeff, and Linda are all considered desirable and positive, while Agatha, Edgar, Mabel, and Phoebe provoke an opposite reaction. Names can also affect the way people behave and how they feel about themselves. One of the most common habits is to name a son after the father and use "Jr." as part of the son's name. The practical problem, of course, is differentiating between father and son, but the real difficulty lies in the son's feeling of sharing an identity with someone else, having to compete with his father for recognition, or going through life with unmistakably lesser status.

There is little question that names help shape our personalities. Even though they are an important force in our lives affecting our development, we can't help wondering how we would have turned out if our names had been different. For example, would Donald J. Trump be as equally famous if his name were Adolphus J. Trumpenstein?

In a previous discussion we stated how regrettable it is that one has no say in the choice of parents. As disappointing as that may be, a further frustration in early life is not being able to choose your own name. What you are called is determined shortly after confirmation of your mother's pregnancy. You are not even born yet and you're already late to the party. You might think your name should be Robert or Michael or John, but suddenly you're expected to respond to Broderick or Demarcus or even Thaddeus, for God's sake.

Regardless of the name they choose, parents should be held liable for creating names that utterly defy easy spelling. We're talking about names like Saoirse, Dwayne, and Dashiell, for example, as well as Jaden, which is also spelled Jaydin, Jaidyn, Jaydon, Jaiden, Jadyn and Jadon. Can you imagine what poor Jaden will go through for the rest of his life? "No, for the third time," he will say, "there is no 'y' in my name." And as for Cindy or Cyndi, as well as Brandy or Brandi, who on earth really cares? Another bad habit of naming is using androgynous names, those that apply equally to both sexes, such as Lee, Terry, Casey, Riley, or Pat. I once was invited by a person named Sam O'Leary to meet for tea at the Savoy Hotel in London. When I arrived the place was overflowing with women. After a few nervous moments a lovely young woman came up to me and said, "Hello, I'm Samantha O'Leary. You see what I mean? How was I to know Sam was Samantha, not Samuel?

Parents have also committed severe blunders by trying to be amusing in naming their offspring. Bill Lear, for example, founder of Lear Jet, named his second daughter Chanda. That's right, Chanda Lear, like the hanging light over the dining room table. And that's just the tip of the weird-naming iceberg. The following are a sample of actual names created by the twisted imagination of parents who either didn't realize the perpetual hell they were creating for their child, or simply believed they were just too clever for words.

Let's start with the Case's son Justin—Justin Case. Then there's Adam Baum, Frank N. Stein, Sam Minella, Moe Lester (say it fast), Lily Pond, Dinah Soares (think tyrannosaurus rex), Brandi Glass, Warren Peace, Emma Royds (ouch), Paige Turner, and Iona Corolla, who probably drives a Ford.

At the extreme end of naming depravities has to be Mr. and Mrs. Jackson, who named their first-born Tonsillitis, who, along with his brother Meningitis, helped care for sisters Laryngitis, Appendicitis, and Peritonitis. This is not intended as a joke, only a warning to those tempted to commit similar child-abuse.

For all of you who were made the butts of your parent's lame jokes, here's the good news: you're not stuck with that screwball name forever. Many people change their names later in life for a variety of reasons, and so can you. Do you think Woody Allen got his name from Gepetto? No way—his name was originally Allen Konigsberg, which he changed at the first opportunity. And Samuel Langhorne Clemens, while piloting steamboats on the Mississippi prior to embarking on a literary career, became Mark Twain. Similarly, Jonathan Leibowitz became the comedian Jon Stuart, Archibald Leach turned into the suave actor Cary Grant, and Erich Weiss magically became the famous Harry Houdini.

The list goes on and on as more people become sick and tired of dealing with the burden of their ill-conceived names. They recognize they have a choice to do whatever is necessary to correct imperfections imposed on them by others.

Popular bands years ago were generally named for their leaders, such as Tommy Dorsey, Benny Goodman, and Glenn Miller. But after big bands went the way of the dinosaurs, new groups searched for original and memorable fictitious names, a practice that continues to this day. Amazingly, first attempts often failed miserably, such as the Beach Boys, who were originally known as the Pendletons, a name associated with the plaid wool shirts favored by the surfing community. Similarly, Simon and Garfunkel as teenagers took the name Tom and

Jerry, despite the name's connection to the cartoon characters. Having little success, they reverted to their real names as adults and, as they say, the rest is history.

So it went with the Screaming Abdabs, who became Pink Floyd, the Salty Peppers, who ended up as Earth, Wind, and Fire, and Gene Simmons's group, Wicked Lester, who later switched to the name Kiss.

Studies have shown that people prefer names that are simple to pronounce and understand. Beyond that criterion most favor shortened versions of names, like Joe for Joseph, Tom for Thomas, and Nan for Nancy. But how do you account for using the name Bob for Robert, Bill for William, and Dick for Richard? Those shortened names seem totally disconnected from the longer versions. Why then, by the same arbitrary reasoning, shouldn't someone named Demetrius be called Zeke? It makes just about as much sense.

Certain names that are based on one's ethnicity, religion, or background often provoke discrimination. Most Americans are not consciously racist, but every so often bigotry rears its ugly head. For example, job applicants with names like Susan or Richard needed to send about ten resumes to get one callback, while those with names like Latisha or Abdulla needed to send fifteen or more resumes to get one callback. Those whose names sound African-American, Muslim, or even Hispanic often find it harder to get a job. They are twice as likely as whites to be unemployed and are paid nearly twenty-five percent less when they are employed. Although most Americans deny harboring racist thoughts, ignorant beliefs are sometimes activated as a result of one's name.

A recent study supported the assertion that children receiving ethnic-type names have more difficult lives than those receiving more traditional names. So what is a Shanika, Ahmed, or Gabriela to do? In some cases they simply Anglicize their names. Mohammed becomes "Mo," and Sameer become "Sam". Others, frankly, are proud of their names and believe that when they excel in life the public will embrace their success and ignore their less traditional names. Thus, Barack Hussein Obama, a name many have trouble spelling, became the 44th President of the United States. An odd circumstance surrounds the situation of Mohammad Ali and Kareem Abdul-Jabbar, two of the most celebrated sports figures of the 20th century. Born Cassius Clay and Lew Alcindor respectively, both converted to Islam, which included the name changes. Ali became a professional boxer and activist, while Jabbar recently received the Presidential Medal of Freedom, the Nation's highest civilian honor. Despite having unconventional names, some actually transcend discriminatory attitudes and excel beyond one's wildest dreams.

Most Americans have a problem with the pronunciation of foreign names, for example, Przybyla, Ejiofor, and Pavlyuchenkova. These tongue twisters recall Al Capp's cartoon character, Joe Btfsplk, who brought disastrous misfortune to everyone around him. He always appeared with a black cloud over his head, and not incidentally, always got a laugh. Some names as well, become famous simply because they are ridiculous and unforgettable. Groucho (actually born Julius) Marx's movie characters were variously named Rufus T. Firefly, Otis P. Driftwood, and Quincy A. Flagstaff. And one of comedian Red (actually born Richard) Skelton's great characters was Clem Kadiddlehopper.

So, returning to the question of "What's in a name?" we see that Juliet's point of view may have been logical, but there is much more about names to consider. Names evoke images, and some images are more favorable than others. "Ethan", for example is much softer sounding than "Rocco". And whom would you prefer to pick a fight with, "Aaron" or "Spike"?

A young friend once decided to become a country western singer. He chose the stage name "Buck Grant,", which was about as far from his real name as Portugal is from New Zealand. The name worked brilliantly, bringing great attention, curiosity, and audiences. Unfortunately, my friend was a less than distinguished performer, and his career came to an end shortly after his initial concert. But he loved the new name, and when he later drifted into the more suitable profession of accounting the sign on the door read "Buck Grant, CPA".

Pets

The world consists of pet lovers, pet non-lovers, and those who look upon pets with indifference. Clearly, I am one of the latter. My earliest experience with pets began when I was eight years old and purchased a white mouse from a friend at the bargain price of ten cents. The friend's mother had declared that either the mouse had to go or my friend would become a homeless waif. The mouse was about four inches long, with a tail of equal length. He had rounded ears, and was pure white, except for his pink eyes. My friend had named him Elmer, as in Elmer Fudd, but I renamed him Mickey in honor of Mr. Disney's popular creation. If Elmer resented the name change, he never let on.

Mickey lived in a galvanized metal pail that I filled with shredded newspapers. The pail provided ample room for his activities and was tall enough to be escape-proof. I fed him table scraps, mostly vegetables surreptitiously scraped off my dinner plate, and we played for a short time nearly every day. I would take him out of his pail, and he would run up and down my arm and often sit on my shoulder. It was in no way a polished carnival act, but Mickey appeared to enjoy the exercise as much as I.

My love affair with Mickey ended tragically one morning, and later that day I wrote a poem to memorialize the event. Please remember, I was eight years old.

I had a pet whose name was Mickey,
He was very small but oh so tricky,
One morning I arose and looked in his pail,
And there was Mickey, deader than a doornail.

Okay, I realize it's not Tennyson, Longfellow, or even William McGonagall, widely acclaimed as the worst poet in the history of the world, but it explains what happened, even if the sorrow and anguish are only marginally implied.

A few years later we had a dog for a short while. Having another pet was not my idea, but rather the notion of my aggressive brother. He insisted on having an attack dog, one that would tear to shreds anyone who dared threaten him. He settled on such a pet because our parents refused to allow in the house his first choice–a Thompson submachine gun. The Thompson became infamous during the Prohibition era, as it was popular with both law enforcement officers and criminals. Also known as a "Tommy Gun", "The Chopper", and "Chicago Typewriter", the weapon appealed to my brother's elevated level of hostility.

Our dog was a terrier of one sort or another and was all beige in color, except for black-tipped ears and tail. So my imaginative brother named him Tippy. Out of lack of respect for both my brother and the pet I referred to him as Tipsy.

My parents were neutral about having a dog, especially an attack dog, but whatever resistance they had faded when my brother swore on the family bible that he, and he alone, would feed, walk, bathe, and care for the animal. That promise lasted barely two weeks. It was my mother who noticed that Tippy was slowly being starved to death. There had been no food in his dish for days, and the pet was losing weight and walking in circles like some demented patient in a mental hospital.

My mother threatened that if my brother didn't live up to his initial promise Tippy would be history. At that point I don't think my brother really cared, because the docile animal never came close to developing sufficient hostility to become the canine secret weapon he yearned for. Things calmed down for a while, but the family dog began to resent his new home. He acted as though he hated the entire family–who could blame him–and shortly thereafter went into a depression that headed downhill at increasing speed. Tippy became inactive, withdrawn, and would spend hours under a bed.

Two weeks later the despondent animal was returned to the shelter from which he came. Though we were previously told he was unhappy there, compared to our house, his former home probably appeared like the original Garden of Animal Delights. With no hesitation whatever, not even a barked farewell, he bounded out of the car and raced to greet his old buddies. His rejection of our family came as a blow to my brother, who realized that he had failed miserably as a pet owner. When we called out our final farewell, Tippy responded by sniffing the air and running quickly towards a fire hydrant.

My other personal experience with a pet came one summer when we vacationed with my uncle Nathan and his family at Twin Lakes in Wisconsin. My uncle had rented a large guesthouse that was located on a working farm. The place was quickly overflowing with close relatives. My aunt Gracie enjoyed being away from home, but apparently only when everything familiar came along for the ride. So, in addition to her favorite carpet sweeper, carving knife, and waffle iron, she brought along the family pet, a yellow canary named Tweety. You heard right, Tweety–like the sound of a piccolo imitating a songbird.

My cousin Gary, hardly a fan, said, "That's not only a stupid name, that's the most stupid pet in the entire stupid animal kingdom." His mother and two sisters wholeheartedly disagreed; they thought Tweety was an absolute gift from heaven.

During our two weeks in Wisconsin the miserable bird never stopped tweeting. His songs were as endless and annoying as a broken record, and it sounded to my untrained ear like a mentally challenged soprano practicing her scales. The family members who loved the canary acted as if Maria Callas was in the living room, having just dropped by to serenade us. Our only relief was at feeding time, during which Tweety shut up long enough to peck away at his dinner. At the end of each melodious day the canary's cage was covered with a dense cloth, the bird fell asleep on his perch, and the concert was over, only to begin again the next day at the crack of dawn.

A day or two into our second week on the farm I awoke to the mournful wails of several relatives. It was so sorrowful I begin to suspect someone had died. As it turned out someone had. When the cover on the birdcage was removed that morning there was Tweety lying on crumpled newspapers, feet in the air, deader than the embalmed corpse

31

of King Tut lying in his sarcophagus. A passerby might have thought that the country's president had just been assassinated, and a doleful chorus was hired to sob its collective heart out. Believe me, it would have brought tears to your eyes.

That sad day became a Memorial Day of sorts as each of my uncle Nathan's family members recounted loving stories of their precious pet bird. Even Gary, no previous admirer of Tweety, expressed his admiration for the bird. Actually, his tribute came out more like a coal miner voicing appreciation for the canary that just dropped dead, while providing an early warning about noxious gas in the mineshaft.

The next item of business was how to dispose of the yellow-feathered corpse. My cousin Kay suggested we cremate the bird on the barbecue in the rear yard.

"That is truly barbaric," said her sister, Shelley. "I think we should have a formal funeral. Maybe we can find a local rabbi and even a professional cantor."

At this point, my father began to lose it. "A rabbi? A cantor?" repeated my father. "First of all, this is Twin Lakes. The closest rabbi is probably in Chicago! Secondly, It's a bird, for Chrissake–just a goddam dead bird. What's the matter with you people, are you all *meshugenah*?

The lesson I learned that summer was that some people consider pets genuine family members. Whether it's a parrot, goldfish, monkey or python, owners often treat their pets like the perfect child they've always longed for. Pet owners today contribute some fifty billion dollars each year to the pet industry. This includes products and services, like food, training, boarding, and miscellaneous supplies. And what do people receive for that investment? One receives companionship, pleasure, and quite often, a nonjudgmental and loyal best friend.

Some people contend that our love of animals surpasses our concern for people. Sociologists at Northeastern University tested that claim by publishing fake news articles describing different accounts of vicious beatings of a puppy, an adult dog, a human infant, and a human adult. The subjects of the experiment had no idea the articles were bogus, and after reading their stories they were tested on their empathy and the emotional distress felt for the victims. The story in which the victim was a human adult elicited, by far, the lowest level of emotional concern in readers. The "winner" when it came to evoking empathy was not the puppy but the human infant. The puppy, however, came in a close second with the adult dog not far behind.

In another experiment exploring circumstances in which people value animal over human lives, studies found that women care more about animals than do men. In a deadly situation scenario, female subjects were nearly twice as likely as males to say they would save a dog over a person. The conclusion seems to be that, at least sometimes, we do value animals over people.

There are exceptions, of course, like the friend who never fails to mention how useless our current pet cat appears to be. "She's always asleep," he says, "Doesn't she ever go out and catch a mouse?"

"She's getting too old for that," I reply.

"You might say she's at an awkward age", he says; "too old to be cute, but not dead yet."

We share the earth with roughly 40,000 other vertebrate animals, but most of us are only concerned over the treatment of a handful of species. And while most deeply love their pets, there is little hue and cry over the two dozen horses that die each week at racetracks in the United States and the horrific treatment of the nine billion chickens we consume every year. As environmental philosopher Chris Diehm points out, *"There is a paradox of the cats in our houses and cows on our plates."*

And now a few words about service pets: In 2010, the U.S. Department of Justice declared that: *"Service animals are pets that are individually trained to do work or perform tasks for people with disabilities"*. Examples include guiding blind people, alerting deaf people, pulling a wheelchair, protecting a person having a seizure, or performing other duties. Service animals are working animals, not pets. Similarly, an emotional support animal (ESA) is a companion animal, determined by a medical professional, to provide benefit for an individual with a range of physical, psychiatric, or intellectual disabilities.

The result of these new regulations has opened a floodgate of abuse where pets are now permitted by law to wander through restaurants, attend concerts, and sit side-by-side with their owners on airplanes. All that is required is the claim, supported by a medical document, that one's creature is a licensed companion necessary to their mental well-being. Detractors ask, "What about the mental well-being of everyone else?"

During a recent test case a reporter carried a fifteen-pound, thirteen-inch-long turtle that was tethered to a leash. Verifying it was an emotional-support animal, the reporter gained admission to tour an art museum. Later the reporter and his pet turtle visited a hair salon, shoe store, and finally a delicatessen. At no point was the odd pair denied access. Even more shocking were subsequent adventures by the same reporter with a snake, turkey, pig, and alpaca. Apparently no power is mightier than that of a certified ESA pet.

It is quite common for owners to outlive their pets, since the life span of hamsters is about three years, while cats and dogs rarely live for more than fifteen years. Therefore, if you wish your pet to survive longer than you, and avoid the depressing, funereal days that lie ahead, you are advised to start with a tortoise or an Asian elephant.

Undomesticated animals, such as lions, tigers, and bears, generate a fascination, as well as fear, in most people. As long as they remain caged in a zoo they are magnificent to behold. But the current trend is to let them live free in their native habitat and observe them, camera in hand, from the safety of a Range Rover.

Not many years ago hunting safaris allowed those with the means to hunt, shoot, and carry off the remains of dead wild animals. Some can still be seen adorning trophy rooms in private estates. They always appear high on the wall, as if they've suddenly crashed through, stopped only by their broad shoulders.

Killing wild animals has become less popular, as we have developed more respect for diminishing species. Like bullfighting, it's a pastime that will soon fade away as more people realize it is preferable for us all to co-exist. Now, if we could only convey that concept among xenophobic citizens, religious extremists, and political parties.

Cars

Every 15-year-old kid of my generation—most girls included—could hardly wait to turn sixteen and get a driver's license. A driver's license didn't mean you'd suddenly go out and buy a car; few had the money for that. It simply meant you could borrow the family car—when available—and get that amazing sense of independence that comes from zooming off by yourself to wherever that incredible machine would take you. Driving represented a coming of age, the first genuinely adult responsibility, and an escape from parental rules and regulations. It was freedom personified.

Most of us learned driving basics from a friend or relative who ground down tooth enamel gritting through tense lessons on empty side streets. Once having learned the essentials we spent endless hours driving up and down the driveway practicing shifting—clutch, gas, brakes, and so forth—while avoiding destruction of the hedge or flower bed bordering the narrow concrete path.

On the morning of my sixteenth birthday I was up at dawn waiting for the Department of Motor Vehicles office to open. I had read the Driver's Handbook so many times I committed to memory everything in it, from the required parking distance from a railroad track (7-½ feet) to the illegal blood alcohol concentration level of a driver (0.08% or more). That was the easy part. My real concern was the driving test itself.

My father drove me to the DMV Office that fateful morning, and an officer, whose nametag read "Percival Smiley", was assigned to us.

But Smiley was not smiling. In fact, he had the unpleasant expression of someone who truly despised his job.

"Pleased to meet you," I said amiably, trying to break the ice. There was no response. "Percival's an unusual name," I continued. "Do people call you Percy?"

I knew at once I had made a terrible mistake.

"That's really not your concern," he answered brusquely. "To you, I'm Officer Smiley. Let's get going." That's all I needed; I was already as nervous as a turkey in November. I stuck my arm straight out the window to signal pulling away from the curb, and off we went. Smiley gave terse directions as we headed towards a busy intersection.

"Turn left," he said. Then, "Turn right and back into that empty space at the curb." The space appeared shorter than the car, but I managed to squeeze in on the first try. Fabulous job, I thought, but Smiley remained mute. He continued making notes and rarely looked up. Only once did he offer a comment, and that was to caution that one of my right turns was a bit wide.

For about twenty minutes my innards churned, but my concentration never wavered. I kept well within the speed limit, braked cautiously, signaled properly, and never uttered a single word. After what felt like the 24 Hours of Le Mans, we approached the DMV Office. It was like crossing the finish line.

"Okay," said Officer Smiley.

Okay? Just okay? What the hell did that mean? Okay I passed, or okay the driving test is over and you failed miserably. I thought I did pretty well, but Smiley acted like I just ran over an old lady crossing the street in a wheelchair.

"How did he do?" asked my father. Again, Smiley said, "Okay."

As it turned out, I passed the driving test and got my license. I never saw Percival Smiley again, but the memory of that day forever defined for me "mixed emotions".

I did not have a car of my own until I was twenty-four years old. I had completed my education, spent over a year traveling the world on a fellowship, and was now home looking for my first architectural job. I was dead broke, and with money owed, my total net worth was a negative number. My father was about to purchase a new car, and he suggested I take his old car and pay it off when I began earning money. The car was a 1950 four-door Chevrolet sedan in the most bilious shade of lime green ever conceived by a Detroit designer. I truly hated that car, but there was no other option. Drive the huge, ugly Chevy, take a bus, or walk.

I was embarking on a career in architecture, I had lofty design ambitions, and here I was, driving one of the most repugnant products to ever come out of the General Motors Technical Center. As far as I was concerned that Chevy was equivalent to the disastrous Ford Edsel that appeared a few years later. It was a total embarrassment. When driving to work I often wore a cap pulled down over my ears. And to avoid humiliation I parked on the street most of the time, rather than the company parking lot. A fellow designer suggested I paint the car black. "It won't be nearly as noticeable," he said, "and basic black is actually kind of fashionable these days."

I had an even better idea. I traded in the Chevy after a few months, went into greater debt, and bought a brand new 1954 convertible MG-TF. It was a classic English design that I first saw while in college. A fellow architectural student had an MG-TC from the late 1940s. I thought it was the most stunning car I'd ever seen. By the early 1950s MGs were being built to U.S standards and exported to America by the scores.

The MG (Morris Garages) factory was sold in 1981, and today there are virtually none of their products on the road, not even in Great Britain. So it's probable you've never seen this remarkable car. Let me describe it. It was a small, compact, and elegant racing-style car that could go 85 miles-per-hour if you were heading slightly downhill. The body was painted a delicate shade of gray with a hint of green, and the seats were covered in red leather. The convertible top and tonneau cover were black canvas, and the grille, body trim, and hubcaps were sparkling chrome.

The car seated two people, preferably slender friends, as the five-foot total width of the car positioned the seats quite close together. In addition, when operating the four-speed manual gearshift the driver often grazed the passenger's thigh when shifting into fourth gear. Depending on the passenger's sex, that was not a particular problem. The car was about twelve-feet long and quite low to the ground. You could actually reach down from the driver's seat and touch the pavement, which—while driving—was borderline suicidal.

MGs were almost always driven with the top down, and sometimes with the windscreen folded down, unless you were literally driving through a hurricane. There were no actual side windows, but plastic side curtains were provided and cleverly fitted into the door panels. If you wanted to enclose the car during a genuine storm it would take perhaps ten minutes or more to put up the top and install the side curtains. By then you were soaked, and the car became a sauna on wheels that was soon fogged up and painfully claustrophobic.

There were several other shortcomings, or "eccentricities", as MG owners rationalized them, such as no heater, no radio, no gas gauge, and virtually no storage. To be honest, the car was as irritating as a friend who is late to every event, unapologetic, and oblivious to the discomfort of others. But, as a driver, you forgave all that, because it was a thrill to drive and even a greater thrill to own an attractive and truly marvelous automobile. MG owners felt a close kinship to one another, and when passing, one customarily waved modestly to the other MG driver in a move similar to a half salute.

I had many cars after the MG, but none was as gratifying or delightful to own as that first car. I drove my MG for eight years and nearly 100,000 miles. It was frustrating when some electrical or mechanical malfunction occurred, which happened more frequently as time went on, but eventually I realized it was a sensitive machine, and I dealt with it patiently, not unlike one would deal with an obstreperous two-year-old.

I was forced to give up my MG when our first-born no longer fitted comfortably on the narrow shelf behind the seats. I realized the kid needed a strapped-in seat. It was time to replace the car and move on. I truly loved that car as much as anyone could love an inanimate object; and when I think of it today I realize how lucky I was to have had the experience–frustrations and all–of driving a refined and amazing automobile.

I sold my MG to an old school friend, who had coveted it for years. Two weeks later the transmission gave out, requiring a complete replacement. That happened decades ago, but the friend has never let me forget it. "Now about that pile of crap you sold me," he usually begins.

Driving these days is no longer the fun it once was. When I bought my first car the population in Los Angeles was under two million, whereas today it's about double that. Yet few streets have been added since then, so every street has more than twice as many vehicles and probably double the number of stoplights as before. Getting around the city has become a painful experience, and the modern freeway system is rarely a better choice. If it's not a jackknifed big-rig clogging traffic, it's a fender-bender blocking half the lanes.

It's also clear that, though cars have become more reliable, drivers have become considerably less so. Some continue to speak on their cell phones or text while traveling at dangerous speeds. A few others think nothing of weaving their way down the road as if the three-martini lunch had no effect on their competence. The most critical offenders, however, are the aggressive drivers–those who deliberately put people and property at risk. Some reckless fools get behind the wheel of a car and turn into hostile warriors, whose every trip is a belligerent foray through enemy lines. Aggressive driving involves speeding, running red lights, tailgating, cutting off other drivers, and weaving through traffic. A particular resentment of mine is reserved for those who fail to use turn indicators, as though informing cars behind them about their next move is classified top-secret. I mean, really, how difficult is it to move one small finger as a courtesy to others?

Any hostile action while driving can lead to road rage, which is a traffic tantrum that may include rude gestures, verbal insults, or dangerous driving targeted toward another driver in an effort to intimidate or release frustration. Road rage can result in altercations or collisions that may cause physical injuries or even death.

Young adults these days are considerably less excited about driving than previous generations. Some don't consider a car necessary, and many haven't even bothered to get a driver's license. They prefer to dial up Uber, use public transportation, or ride with a parent or friend. This development is becoming a major concern for the auto industry, whose products have never before failed to seduce young drivers. But many of today's youngsters consider cars an unnecessary responsibility; they're expensive to own and repair and the cost of gas, insurance, and upkeep is as painful as repaying a student loan. Who needs all that?

The expense of parking is another problem that those without cars will never face. Those costs have gone crazily upward, along with appreciation of land values almost everywhere. Parking in Midtown Manhattan, the most expensive U.S. city in which to park, now runs more than $500 per month. I suppose a Londoner would view that as a bargain, since parking in that city costs twice as much.

The latest automotive development is the self-driving car, which has gone from being a sci-fi fantasy to an emerging reality with the potential to transform the way we live. Automakers and tech companies are racing to put driverless cars on the road within a few years, and they predict that by 2025 every car on the road will be autonomous. Becoming a nation of passengers is a monumental change few can even comprehend. Without a need for a driver's license, the age of sixteen will no longer be a demarcation between childhood and adulthood, a move that will liberate children who will be able to "drive" as soon as their parents allow them to go unsupervised. Parents, meanwhile, will no longer spend hours schlepping their kids from here to there.

Professional taxi drivers, bus drivers, and truckers will be out of a job, and auto-body shops will become 24-hour businesses, so that when your car needs a tune-up, it can take itself to the shop while you're asleep and return before you're awake.

The interior of self-driving cars will also evolve to resemble the first-class section of a jet, or a personal office, with fully reclining seats and built-in entertainment systems. Imagine watching a movie on a big screen, playing a video game, or perhaps listening to a Beethoven symphony while your car takes you effortlessly to work. The self-driving car could also become a comfortable, rolling bedroom, so that one may plan long overnight trips or perhaps park, make love, and save the cost of a motel room. It seems to me that cars of the future may possibly become more fun than staying home.

It is also predicted that in the near future you may not even own your car. Hailing a driverless car on demand is the likely future of local transportation. If, however, you do buy, you may decide to share the vehicle by renting it out when it's not in use.

Perhaps the greatest advantage of driverless cars is the elimination of fatal traffic accidents, which now take more than 30,000 American lives annually. Researchers estimate that driverless cars could, by midcentury, reduce traffic fatalities by up to 90 percent. Thus, driverless cars may rank among the most transformative public-health initiatives in human history. There is reason to be optimistic about the technological future of cars.

But one can't help feel a sad loss for future generations who will never know the thrill of driving an MG-TF on a curving country road, with top down, wind in your hair, and a silly grin on your face.

Art

There is an eatery in our neighborhood called Art's Delicatessen, and the sub-title on the sign outside says, *"Every sandwich is a work of Art"*. Clever, you must admit, but it has nothing to do with the kind of art I have in mind. I'm talking about fine art, the kind of art you see in a gallery or museum. Before attending college I knew little about art. I was aware of the obvious icons, like the Mona Lisa and Whistler's mother, and I also admired Saturday Evening Post covers by Norman Rockwell and provocative pin-ups painted by Vargas and Petty in Esquire magazine. But people said that wasn't art; that was illustration. Who cared? In those days I didn't know the difference. Years later Hugh Hefner offered us heavenly females wearing little more than what they were born with, and many considered that development one of the loftiest expressions of visual art.

So, I continued to wonder, what *is* art? Everyone had an answer to that question, and each answer was as different as every snowflake. I figured artistic disagreements would probably continue forever. Regardless of what you personally believe to be a stunning work of art, be prepared to hear someone say, "You can't be serious! You call that art? My eighty-year-old grandmother, glaucoma and all, could do better."

Art, like politics and religion, is among the most controversial of all subjects. Experts on the subject say that art is a creative expression that generates an emotional response. It's a universal language that conveys powerful visions beyond the capacity of words. Art is also a reflection of one's culture and often generates admiration, happiness, and delight, as well as confusion, revulsion, and outright hostility.

That's Life

Before the advent of photography, people and things were represented through drawings, paintings, mosaics, stained glass, and statues. The church recognized centuries ago that images, like Leonardo da Vinci's *Last Supper*, taught important biblical lessons to those unable to read. Paintings were also used to record historical events, like Bonaparte Crossing the Alps by Jacque-Louis David or the Death of Socrates by the same artist. Paintings such as Gilbert Stuart's several portraits of George Washington allow us to know what our first president looked like. Those unfamiliar with that image can take a dollar bill out of their wallets and, there he is, the father of our country looking back at us, as he has been for more than a hundred years.

One of the original Stuart portraits of Washington hangs in the National Portrait Gallery in our nation's capitol with the title beneath that says, "Gilbert Stuart", which led a friend to remark, "It's amazing! The guy's the spitting image of George Washington."

It is generally agreed that the "Mother of all Arts" is architecture, a subject with which I have firsthand knowledge. Cave painting may have preceded the practice of architecture, but the latter is considered the "mother" because it embodies every other art. All people—even homeless ones—experience architecture every single day. And though engineers and builders have the technical knowledge to assemble buildings, it is the architect who has the training, sensitivity, and talent to actually design buildings that have lasting value as art.

Most non-architects rarely appreciate what goes into a well-planned and beautifully proportioned building sitting harmoniously on its site. Few may realize why they are able to move easily from one space to another or why the shape and proportions of a particular space feel comfortable. The emotional pleasure or discomfort of a space is a result of a designer's choice with regard to form, scale, light, and other such considerations.

With obvious advantages in employing an architect, it's curious why so many fail to use their services. It is estimated that architects design only ten to fifteen percent of all new houses. That's not only bad news for architects, but worse news for the aesthetics of most neighborhoods. Many people are unable to see the difference between a well-designed structure and one that is truly unattractive. Most know when something is physically uncomfortable, because it results in an ache or pain. But visual discomfort is often unnoticed because many are visually insensitive—if not for all intents and purposes—blind. Although most shelter magazines feature beautifully designed interiors, many readers remain unaffected. Their homes are often a visual disaster, with mismatched, uncomfortable furniture, morbid color schemes, and dreadful artwork on the walls. Clearly, many people don't realize—or perhaps don't care—how terrible things look.

A serious problem is that many furnishings for sale—couches, lamps, tables, and chairs—are poorly designed, and that's where the problem begins. Sadly, too few classic designs are available, and as in other fields, most of what is produced lacks artistic merit. Thus, what is available in stores severely limits the store buyer's options—even assuming the buyer has impeccable taste.

If, however, you sat in an Eames lounge chair or a Le Corbusier armchair, you would realize at once the difference between good and bad design. There is nothing as pure as a chair in the classic Shaker style or the beauty of a Thonet bentwood chair from more than a hundred years ago. They are sill available today, so why settle for less?

As we all know, everyone is an art critic: "I may not know anything about art," they say, "but I know what I like." With architecture, they contend: "I not only know what I like, but I know plenty about how it should be put together. So who needs an expensive architect? I'll sketch out a plan and let my builder figure it out." I have been presented with such sketches, and they are, in general, amateurish, unrealistic, and shockingly bad. If the same client decided to bypass the surgeon and perform his or her own appendectomy it's off to the mortuary faster than you can say, "Do-it-yourself has real limitations."

While studying the history of architecture in school we inevitably came across classic art, since architects throughout the ages were often painters and sculptors as well. The most remarkable of these was Michelangelo Buonarroti, a triple threat talent who designed the massive dome of St. Peters in Rome, painted the biblical figures on the Sistine Chapel ceiling, and sculpted the magnificent statue of David. Others, like Giotto, designed the glorious bell tower at the Florence Cathedral and also painted the masterful frescoes in Assisi. Renaissance men were often artists, poets, and musicians, as well as scientists, mathematicians, and inventors. Leonardo da Vinci, for example, dabbled impressively in every one of those activities.

Some people today believe that art is passé and truly unimportant. They are the ones who have no guilt whatever in eliminating art classes from elementary schools to save a few education dollars. As a result, many of today's younger generation have grown up with little knowledge or appreciation for the visual arts. The trite, sentimental, and amateurish works that hang on many living room walls is ample evidence of this phenomenon. Some work is so bad, one suspects it's only there to cover a hole in the plaster. Mediocre art is everywhere, and most people are oblivious to it. The Canadian painter, Robert Genn, once said, *"The oceans of art are awash with people who cannot paint. This is a condition that would not be tolerated in other professions, such as Medicine, Dentistry or among members of the Airline Pilot's Association."*

On the other hand, since art is more or less subjective, many believe it's up to the viewer to judge whether or not it has merit. Some believe that if the majority loves something it must have value. Others reply that the majority is often wrong, since, as the American author, Thomas Sturgeon declared, *"Ninety percent of everything is crap."* This notion has become so popular it is now known as Sturgeon's Law. Even George Bernard Shaw got into the act with his observation, *"If more than ten percent of the people like a painting, you can be sure it's bad."*

Ironically, more museums than ever are being created these days to display both public and private collections. If you were to visit a local museum's gift shop and purchase an inexpensive reproduction from their collection, and then hang that piece on your wall, you would probably do the artist, the museum, and yourself a giant favor.

Nonrepresentational, or abstract art is another subject that provokes remarkable hostility. The common response by the uninitiated ranges from, "What the hell do you call that?" to "In my opinion the fire extinguisher hanging next to it is prettier."

When I first became aware of abstract painters, like Miro, Kandinsky, and Mondrian, I found them pleasing, but I failed to understand them. Then one day a professor suggested, "You probably don't understand the song of a bird either, but it can often be a beautiful experience. You don't have to understand art or music or even a full moon to be moved emotionally. So why not give it a chance?" And so I gave it a chance and now, years later, feel enriched by embracing works by Ellsworth Kelly, Josef Albers, Andy Warhol, and others whose lithographs I own.

My first purchase of serious art came early in life when traveling on my post-graduation fellowship. Walking along the Seine one morning with an artist friend I noticed a lithograph in an antique store window that looked similar to the drawings of Toulouse-Lautrec, the famous artist whose work captured the spirit of the Moulin Rouge.

"It can't be," said my friend. "First of all, few Lautrecs are available these days, and no idiot would display one sitting in full sunlight in a junk shop window."

The drawing was titled *Etude de Femme,* and it showed a model undressing in a bedroom. The lithograph was signed, numbered, and dated from 1893. The proprietor insisted it was absolutely genuine. I was a bit suspicious when learning the sales price was seventy-five dollars. Seventy-five dollars in those days would amount to perhaps ten times that today. Still, a Lautrec lithograph of that type today would be worth thousands of dollars. Actually, the point was moot; as a struggling student I felt fortunate to have just enough to avoid sleeping under the Pont Neuf at night, with enough left over to purchase coffee and a croissant each morning. The proprietor and I, with the Lautrec in hand, walked a few blocks to visit an expert who could validate the authenticity of the work. Within twenty minutes he assured us this was the real thing. I wired my parents to borrow the necessary money, and on the following day became owner of a lovely lithograph that has brought me endless years of visual pleasure.

Emboldened by that experience and despite being up to my eyeballs in debt, one week later I purchased another lithograph from the gallery representing Henri Matisse. Matisse was still alive at that time, so the price was a reasonable thirty-five dollars. With little hesitation I borrowed that amount from a friend, and despite flirting with debtor's prison, became owner of a beautiful female head described by the few black lines.

"Collect what you love", advised a professional collector, "because if no one else on earth likes it, it will be yours forever". Of course, some trade artworks like common stocks; they hold a piece until it appreciates in price and then dump it for the profit. As far as I'm concerned these are not collectors, they are speculators. Not that there's anything wrong with speculation, but I believe dealing with art should be a bit more meaningful than trading pork bellies.

The world of artistic expression is vast, and those wishing to be a part of that world should be prepared for a life of struggle, rejection, and poverty. Whether you paint, act, dance, play an instrument, or write poetry the odds of success are stacked against you. While some artists achieve phenomenal success, most do not. Sadly, that's life. On the other hand, those of us who are attracted to a more creative way of life really don't care. "Fame and fortune are not everything," a friend once said. "There's also disappointment, obscurity, and poverty."

It is my opinion that creative people are truly the lucky ones; there is no greater satisfaction than living a creative life. Franklin Delano Roosevelt once said, *"Happiness lies in the joy of achievement and the thrill of creative effort."* So, as trite as this advice has become, if you do what you love, chances are, you will love what you do. And if so doing you provide aesthetic joy and satisfaction to others, you are doubly blessed.

Romance

They say that falling in love is wonderful
It's wonderful, so they say
And the thing that's known as romance
is wonderful, wonderful, in every way, so they say

The prolific songwriter, Irving Berlin, summed it up perfectly; falling in love *is* wonderful, and many of those who've experienced "the thing that's known as romance" believe it may be even more wonderful–in every way.

Ah, romance–the feeling of excitement and mystery associated with love. Who can forget that feeling when first smitten by love for the object of your affection? Every love song and every Valentine seem to be written with you in mind. The world is suddenly different. There's a spring in your step, you may be humming, you're certainly smiling more, and everyone seems a whole lot nicer. You've never been so happy.

Scientists have discovered that "crazy in love" is not just an expression. Chemical changes occur in the brain of love-struck people causing a lack of good judgment and often, obsessive, irrational behavior. You go out of your way, doing things outside your comfort zone, to make your partner happy. When you're apart you wonder why the phone doesn't ring. And when it does, you speak for hours. You can't wait to be together again. And when you are, you never want it to end. It's thrilling, amazing, a little crazy, and absolutely magical. But all of this is for a higher biological purpose; that is, making reproduction more likely. Being crazy in love is exciting, addictive, confusing, and most will tell you, totally worth it.

My first romance–some might call it infatuation–happened when I was nine years old. Yes, nine. Don't smirk; it's possible. Only five years earlier I discovered an incredible fact of life. I was perplexed about how one knew if a newborn was a boy or girl. You must remember that before Google, before everyone knew everything, and since I had no sister, little kids like me were bewildered by things like that. All I knew was that boys had short hair and girls had long hair, but most babies had no hair. So what's the deal? And then it was explained to me. The difference between boys and girls, as it turned out, was more than hair–much more.

What I learned on that fateful day was the start of a sexual education on a subject that continues to fascinate me. By the time I was nine and in the fourth grade at Avondale elementary school in Chicago I began to notice Anna Polanski, the cutest girl in our class. It didn't even matter that Anna hardly knew I was alive, or so I assumed. Then came the dramatic day my father announced we were moving to California. No more Chicago, no more Avondale, and no more fantasies about Anna Polanski.

On my last day in school our teacher, Miss Rosengarten, gave me a small going-away party. As she announced to the class that I'd be leaving I heard a voice say, "Oh no!" Believe it or not, the exclamation came from Anna. Not only was she aware of me, she seemed to care that I was leaving. Later she confessed, "I'll miss you, but I'd like to give you my address and maybe you can send me a postcard from California. Maybe one with a lot of palm trees."

Interpret that as you will, but to me it was the equivalent of, "I will miss you, I want to stay in touch with you, and oh–by the way–I'm deeply in love with you". It was my first romantic connection and a sentimental arrow aimed straight at my heart. Yes, at the age of nine I fell in love with Anna Polanski, and there was no doubt in my mind she also loved me. We corresponded for a few months, but our geographic incompatibility eventually became an obstacle. Our romantic relationship waned, and in time, Anna became no more than a fond memory. Early on, my insensitive brother referred to my first love as Anna Banana, and thereafter, in retaliation, I referred to him as a stupid, bird-brained dickhead.

High school romances are different, since teenagers are more mature and sexuality becomes the new and exciting focus. Who can possibly forget that first kiss with a willing partner, or the extraordinary strength of will it took to know when to stop? Memories of groping, clinging, and exploring another body remain stronger than most other early recollections. When looking back to those days one can only express gratitude to former partners—as I continue to do—for their affection and generosity.

People meet and fall in love in a variety of ways. At a certain age most are seeking a permanent relationship, one that will lead to marriage and a family. In Colonial times finding a wife was less about romance and more about seeking a woman who could bear children and fulfill the demands of frontier life. Later in history it was the parents who determined their children's future—often without their children's knowledge or approval—based on family connections, politics, or financial arrangements. In many cases the young couple's first meeting was at their wedding ceremony. One can't help imagine what a shock it must have been when the groom lifted his bride's veil. The reactions may have ranged from, "Oh my God" to, "Well, I suppose it could be worse", and an occasional, "Holy crap, she's gorgeous!"

By the early 1900s gentlemen called on potential wives in an effort to better know one another, but it was never without a parent or chaperone in the room. Dating, as we know it today, became popular during the Roaring Twenties when couples went out dancing or perhaps to a movie. It was a time of Prohibition, so of course, everyone drank like fish.

Dating took a holiday during World War II, because most eligible men were otherwise occupied fighting to keep us free. The post-war period was a different story. The birth-control pill was developed, leading to greater sexual activity, abortion became legalized, and women were empowered through the feminist movement.

Dating, hooking up, getting together, hanging out, whatever one calls it, is as popular today as ever, and for many of the same reasons.

That's Life

Most people want companionship, eventually a long-term relationship, and ultimately to raise a family. The methods employed these days to meet the love of one's life is more varied than ever. There are the old standbys, like dating the nice person working in the adjacent cubicle at your office, the gorgeous guy or gal at your gym, or your well-meaning aunt who persists, "Have I got the girl (or guy) for you!" Rarely does Aunt Josephine have someone who'll knock your socks off, but she's well meaning, so you go on another disappointing blind date, vowing never again to fall for your aunt's next great idea.

Believe it or not, some still go to the local bar to meet others of the opposite sex. Even more unbelievably, some guys start the conversation by asking a girl her astrological sign—as if there's a chance he'd be out the door if she said, "Capricorn". Picking up someone at a bar is probably the least favorable way to find romance, unless you're free for only that one night.

One of the great advantages of the Internet Age is online dating. Dozens of sites exist where one may find compatible partners with similar backgrounds, interests, and objectives. One may find the hypothetically, computer-aided perfect match and then meet later for coffee or a drink to see if reality approaches the résumé. Some sites claim to have great success matching men and women, but every so often reality bears little relation to the online puffery, such as, he's married but looking for a little action on the side. She, on the other hand, is deeply in debt and hopes her sexual charm will convince the new boyfriend to bail her out. And then there's the fellow who, as it turns out, doesn't look like his online photo. It's really a picture of his good-looking friend. He also doesn't own the technology company; an uncle on his mother's side does. In fact, he's not even a techie; all he does is answer the phone. Surprise! People sometimes exaggerate, mislead, and outright lie. As they say, "Buyer beware".

Sometimes finding the love of your life is simply a happy accident. Years ago I was employed by a client to add a master suite onto a large, existing house. I was not particularly looking for anything more than a successful design well executed, but I could not help notice that the woman of the house was attractive, personable, and absolutely charming. Over the course of construction we met several times to select finish materials, discuss details, and review progress of the job. After a month or so we began to have lunch occasionally and I noticed we were spending more time discussing subjects that had little to do with the new master suite.

When the project was completed neither of us wanted to say goodbye. The fact is, all we wanted was to be together–forever Unplanned, unintended, and unexpectedly the two of us were soon sharing the new master suite. As I said, happy accidents sometimes happen.

Regardless of how one goes about finding romance, men and women have similar requirements in a mate. Asked to rate their preferences on numerous questionnaires, both men and women agree that high on the list are those who are caring, respectful, positive, and have a sense of humor. It doesn't hurt to be nice-looking either, but everyone defines that differently. Also desirable is a good education, confidence, dependability, generosity, and kindness. Oddly, sexual compatibility was rarely mentioned, though most confessed that was purposely ignored for fear that potential partners might conclude they were sexually obsessed, or worse yet, insatiable. In other words, the average person, both men and women, seek perfection, but being realistic, they are often content to settle for less.

A few idealists find it impossible to settle for less. Some simply cannot bear to compromise when searching for the love of their life. Their models range from fictional lovers, like Romeo and Juliet or Scarlett O'Hara and Rhett Butler to King Edward VIII, who gave up his throne to marry the love of his life, Wallis Simpson. You might point out that seeking an epic romance is generally a matter of rare and extraordinary luck. And they will reply, "Well, why shouldn't it happen to me?" Which is the same question perpetual losers ask about the Powerball lottery.

If most people seeking a mate have specific requirements in mind, and even recognizing that most settle for less than perfection, how do we account for the large number of divorces? About forty percent of all marriages end in divorce, and the reasons are many. Some fall out of love, some were never in love to begin with, and many idealists believe true love lies elsewhere. Over time, people change. The modest bride may become assertive, the successful husband may be revealed as a compulsive gambler, and in some cases love turns to disappointment, frustration, and even loathing.

Many couples fail to realize that good relationships require understanding, compromise, and considerable work. Couples often move in together to test the limits of their compatibility, and some are surprised to discover he likes to go to sleep at ten, whereas she stays up much later watching late night television. She might also be a neat freak requiring everything in its place, while he drops he underwear anywhere but in the hamper, and the last time he took out the trash was two months ago. The fact that any two people actually get along from the start remains one of life's small miracles.

Little problems can become big problems if two people refuse to acknowledge there's a problem in the first place. Speaking to one another is essential if you want to survive the potholes on the road to true love. Allowing small irritations to fester leads to bitterness and is often the first step in the direction of the divorce court. An old New Yorker cartoon says it all. A couple sits at opposite ends of the dinner table and the unhappy husband says, *"It's not the spinach soufflé Edna, it's the last twelve years."*

Many people who write emails or notes often include Os and Xs, indicating hugs and kisses. That's very nice, but much nicer are actual hugs and kisses. Over the years some couples lose the habit of hugging and kissing and hardly realize what they're missing. My personal view is that one should begin and end each day with a generous hug and serious kiss. It's difficult to carry a grudge or be unhappy with someone who makes you feel so physically and emotionally wonderful. Try it and you'll see. As my lifelong partner says, "What does it cost you?" And while you're at it, when was the last time you said to your partner, "I love you"? Try that too, and see how life improves.

Love and romance take courage, and finding the perfect mate may never happen. But one must stay in the game, never surrender, and hope that love will find a way. The alternative is to live a loveless existence, which seems a fairly depressing Plan B.

Food

Food glorious food
What is there more handsome?
Gulped, swallowed or chewed,
Still worth a king's ransom!

So go the Lionel Bart lyrics in the 1960 production of "Oliver" sung by undernourished orphan boys. Fed only gruel, they find comfort imagining a richer menu. We are immediately sympathetic, because lack of food arouses in us the universal fear of death. It is the equivalent of lacking air to breathe. Though "Oliver Twist", the inspiration for the musical, was set in Charles Dickens' London in 1835, today–nearly two hundred years later–thousands of needy families in the U.S. suffer a similar lack of sufficient food.

How is that possible? This is the 21st century; supermarkets are overflowing with every imaginable type of food, and a few dollars will buy fast food in virtually every corner of the country. In addition, an average American family throws away enough food each week to easily feed a family of destitute people. With such an abundance of food how is it possible that anyone still goes to bed hungry?

One explanation might be that most of us who eat regularly have no idea how starvation feels, nor can we appreciate what hungry people suffer. An old joke suggests our inability to empathize:

A homeless panhandler walking along Fifth Avenue in New York approaches a chic, middle-aged woman and says, "Excuse me, Madam, I haven't eaten anything in three days." To which the woman replies, "Oh, what wonderful discipline!"

The problem for most Americans is hardly the lack of food. According to the Center for Disease Control more than half of all adults and a third of all children are overweight or considered obese–which is extremely overweight. There's no question they're getting more than their fair share of food. If any of these people experience pangs of hunger, chances are it's not in their stomachs; it's in their heads. Furthermore, most of these people apparently fail to realize that overindulging often leads to a score of medical problems later in life, including high blood pressure and serious heart problems.

Eating is one of the great pleasure life affords. George Bernard Shaw said, *"There is no love sincerer than the love of food."* We eagerly anticipate each meal, enjoy sharing dinners with friends and family, and look forward with pleasure to attend banquets, celebrations, and any event involving food. Eating is part of the social fabric that binds us together. Even when not particularly fond of your dinner companions, the aroma of a freshly baked pizza will make them seem far more fascinating.

Life was not always that way. Thousands of years ago prehistoric people spent virtually every waking hour searching for food. There were no other activities, interests, or distractions. Life was a battle for survival, and every man and woman was actively engaged in hunting animals or gathering wild greens, nuts, and berries. Perhaps they took an occasional romantic moment to reproduce, but life essentially consisted of finding food while avoiding being eaten by the animals they were pursuing.

Somewhat later, Neolithic tribes developed farming. They grew various crops and domesticated goats, sheep, and pigs, among other animals. By producing their own food, tribes were able to abandon the nomadic life and settle down in permanent communities.

It is interesting to speculate how primitive man determined what was safe to eat. It has been suggested that the first person to eat a raw oyster deserves to be remembered as the bravest human who ever lived. Other foods, as well, must have given pause to those who first discovered them. The lowly potato, for example, didn't first appear like a tantalizing French fry from McDonald's; it had to be dug up, dirt scraped off, and then tasted. Who was the first to do that? Even today some are repelled by the appearance of a tentacle, sweetbread, brain, or liver.

Fortunately, we live in a time of unprecedented food variety. Regardless of the season, fruits and vegetables are available year 'round from all parts of the world. There is also an abundance of foreign food available, representing every part of the planet. If, for example, you're hankering for Peking duck, Mexican tacos, Middle Eastern falafel, or British steak and kidney pie, you can probably find it within a couple of miles from where you live.

A great mystery these days is the number of people who remain truly dreadful cooks. They may be your parents, your best friend, or, God forbid, your spouse. How is it possible that none of those people has ever watched a cooking show on television? Additionally, there are millions of cookbooks sold each year, and the average household has at least a dozen of them at their disposal. It seems to me if you can read, you can become a respectable cook. By merely following the recipe's directions you may even be considered an amazingly talented provider.

Sadly, there are some who have little interest in food, and perhaps no interest at all in cooking. It's a pity, because there is great satisfaction in producing delicious meals. But if you are one of those people whose interests lie elsewhere, and whose talent in the kitchen remains at the "can-barely-boil-water" level, consider buying prepared meals from any number of decent providers, some of whom may even deliver complete meals to your door. And to the truly cooking-challenged, make the world a better place by spending less time in the kitchen and more time in almost any other room in the house. Perhaps your real skill resides in the bedroom.

Close to twenty-five percent of the population eats out at least once a week. The variety of restaurants is mind-boggling as to type, quality, and expense. From neighborhood cafes to gourmet palaces you can find nearly any kind of experience you prefer. Most of us have visited a wide sampling of what is available and, as a result, we are highly opinionated. Most would agree that a restaurant should offer flavorsome food that is well prepared and happily served.

I was once poisoned in a fine restaurant that created their Caesar salad with a raw—and, as it turned out—rotten egg. After an agonizing night I reported the incident the following day to the restaurant, which claimed total innocence.

"Our eggs are fresh each day," insisted the manager.

"Except for the egg in my salad," I replied.

After a few more words, and without being offered even a hint of regret, I hung up and, since then, have put that perilous establishment at the top of my "red alert" list.

Being poisoned in a restaurant today is fairly rare, but other concerns can disturb almost as much. Lighting, for example, in most dining situations should be bright enough so the waiter need not whip out a flashlight for you to read the menu. On the other hand, it should not be as intimidating as the spotlight in the interrogation room down at police headquarters, where one feels the need to confess to almost anything to be set free.

Another peeve is the height relationship of table and chair. One would think that by the 21st century restaurants would get this right. The classic ratio is determined by the height of the person, and that's where the problem begins. Former basketball star, Kareem Abdul Jabbar is more than seven feet in height, while Munchkins in the "Wizard of Oz" were about four and a half feet tall. So how can both be comfortable in a restaurant where the height of tables and chairs are designed for average people? Just as important, if the meal lasts longer than thirty minutes, I believe chair seats should be sufficiently padded. Even sitting in comfortable chairs for an extended period of time simulates, to some degree, weightless effects suffered by astronauts. During the early space age, research revealed that life in zero gravity was linked with accelerated bone and muscle loss and ageing, not to mention perpetual backaches.

Someone once suggested, a party of two is best for enjoying a fine meal—you and your waiter. But if you want a really quiet meal my advice is to turn off the TV and eat at home. Most restaurants are noisy; some playing inappropriate music at such deafening levels that normal conversation is nearly impossible. And if there are groups of six or more surrounding you, expect to suffer noise-induced hearing loss caused by boisterous diners shouting at each other.

Restaurants that appeal to children can result in an even more painful experience. You should know that parents rarely hear sounds emanating from their agitated child, who may continue a hysterical uproar until a parent notices the annoyed stares of surrounding patrons. The International House of Pancakes, or IHOP as it is known, is a particularly fertile venue for such outbursts. It remains a mystery to me that any child can be unhappy in a place where every morsel is covered with sweet syrup and whipped cream. Nevertheless, there have been instances, I am told, where frustrated diners have picked up two buttermilk pancakes from their stack and shoved one into each ear.

Fast food restaurants have gotten a bad rap, in my opinion, because their food is considered unhealthy and excessively fattening—McDonald's being the most ubiquitous example. I once conducted a personal experiment intended to demonstrate that one could eat at such a place regularly and maintain—or even lose—weight. I repeatedly ordered the McChicken sandwich with small fries and diet drink—a meal containing 580 total calories. With the average recommended consumption of 2000 calories a day for an adult man, one could eat that meal three times each day and actually lose weight. I'm not suggesting this represents a well-rounded, healthful diet, or that you should drop everything and rush to McDonald's; but on the other hand, why not? You might be interested to know that McDonald's salads are also a worthwhile consideration. This plug, incidentally, is completely unsolicited.

The beauty of living in a free society is that you can eat whatever you want, whenever you want, and take the consequences as well as the criticism. If the Bistro Shrimp Pasta at the Cheesecake Factory (3120 calories!) floats your boat, dig in. Are you a total vegetarian, organic vegan, sushi fanatic, can't live without pickled herring, or chocolate donuts before bedtime? Who's to say no? Just remember this: A balanced diet has never appeared on an autopsy report as the primary cause of death. Nor did anyone ever blow up to 400 pounds when eating small amounts of everything; yes, every kind and variety of food available, including French fries, caviar, chocolate mousse, and goose liver pate. But here's the caveat: one must eat these foods in strictly modest portions. That's called portion control, a concept many restaurants have forsaken. Those restaurants would do society a healthy favor by serving fewer outrageous mountains of food. Why must patrons, motivated by guilt or greed, be forced to leave a restaurant with a plastic container of leftovers to be eaten cold or soggy the next day? Ugh!

In the past, certain foods have been considered dangerously unhealthy. Eggs, for example, were regarded a few years ago as public enemy number one because of their high cholesterol content. Vigorous campaigns arose to eliminate eggs as though that innocent gift from a chicken might bring back the Bubonic Plague. Today eggs are lauded for being a delicious source of protein. Consumption of other foods as well, such as chocolate, dairy products, nuts, and even potatoes have been compared to flirting with suicide. Those foods are back in favor today, as more research shows they are actually beneficial. The lesson here is to doubt the experts when next they try to eliminate another of your favorite foods.

Finally, a few words about dieting; most diets are a complete waste of time. Many eliminate an entire group of foods until someone comes along with a different group of foods to avoid. Cut your calories and you'll cut your weight. This—I am firmly convinced—works every time. If you need further proof, observe the tragic photos of liberated survivors of the Holocaust. There is not a single overweight person in any cheerless picture. The point is this: Eating less, whether prompted by desire or situation, is a sure way to lose extra pounds. You will also find some advantage if you eat your meals with a salad fork instead of a shovel.

The final word on dieting was expressed years ago by the American chef, Julia Child who said, *"The only time to eat diet food is while you're waiting for the steak to cook."*

Not bad advice.

Nice vs. Nasty

I have a friend—let's call him George—who resembles me in several ways, most faithfully as a compulsive complainer. When I revealed to George, some time ago, my frustration with traffic—that getting from here to there at any time of day—has become increasingly more painful, George had a ready answer. "You call that a problem? Let me tell you about a *real* problem. You want to know the most annoying thing these days? It's just that people are just not nice any more. Politeness is out the window, and no one seems to care. People don't even remember what life was like when you heard words like "please", "thank you", and an occasional "excuse me".

Kindness? Hah! That is so yesterday. Compassion, respect, caring? They're all in the toilet—just got flushed away. No time anymore for sentimental crap like that. Haven't you heard? Politeness is out, rudeness is in; bigotry has replaced tolerance, and bad manners have taken the place of courtesy. It's a goddam jungle out there. Everyone's ready to go to war over every minor slight, and on any day you can see a lot more middle fingers than happy smiles.

People are thoughtless and nasty and no one cares—I mean no one. From our politicians to the inconsiderate jerk next door, there's rarely a kind word. Everyone's into themselves; they just stare at their cell phones all day and rush around trying to be first in line and get one up on everybody else. Honest to God, all you want to do is secede from the human race. I can't even imagine how all this is going to end."

Sad to say, my apoplectic friend had a point. According to recent polls more than half of all people agree that kindness has deteriorated in the past several years; people are more impatient, drivers are more aggressive, and there seems to be a growing acceptance of the rude jerk walking down the street—oblivious to all—talking loudly with a cell phone glued to his ear. You just want to tell him to shut the hell up already.

So what's going on? When did it become acceptable to be disrespectful and rude, and how did human kindness take a back seat to human nastiness? The story actually began with the respectability of the Victorian era. Those were the days when it was universally accepted that, children should be seen, but not heard. Victorian values prescribed that a child's place was to be quiet, well behaved, and do as they were told without question. A popular book at that time, *Table Rules for Little Folks*, cautioned children to, "sit still, be patient and polite, not speak a useless word, and leave quietly when meals are over. Furthermore, interrupting a conversation is forbidden, because children are expected to listen quietly and learn." As a result, children rarely spoke when in the company of adults. Though this strict behavior may have been difficult on children, most adults later referred to it as "the good old days".

The severity of a Victorian upbringing was bound to lead to a more compassionate attitude about child rearing, but change did not appear until the end of World War II. It was Dr. Benjamin Spock's 1946 book, *The Common Sense Book of Baby and Child Care that* created the revolution in parenting. The book sold more than fifty million copies and remains today second only to the Bible in popularity. The book's premise to mothers is that "you know more than you think you do."

As the first pediatrician to study psychoanalysis, Spock's ideas about childcare encouraged parents to be more flexible and affectionate with their children, and to treat them as individuals. He also told his devoted readers that children should not believe their destiny is to serve their family, their country, or their God. They were free, he declared, to set their own aims and pursuits according to their individual inclinations. These revolutionary thoughts were enough to imagine dead Victorians spinning in their graves faster than whirling dervishes.

There were many who criticized Spock for propagating permissiveness and the expectation of instant gratification. Nevertheless, Spock's revolutionary ideas were the beginning of the end for the Victorian notion of children "being seen but not heard". Spock was largely blamed for helping to create the first permissive generation, while also celebrated for bringing about more rational methods of raising children.

Which brings us to today and the popular child-rearing attitude of "self-expression". As an important step in identifying one's true self, the aim of self-expressionism is to allow you to climb out from under that rock, lose your inhibitions and fears, and become the perfect person you were meant to be. Who could argue with that? We all support self-improvement, don't we? Well, not always, and not at any price.

Self-expression extremists occasionally go overboard in the belief that doing whatever they feel like doing at the moment is their inalienable right, regardless of the affect it has on others. Thus, they often feel justified saying anything, behaving anyway, and doing whatever they please in the name of expressing themselves. Worse yet, they expect people to accept them that way. Unbridled self-expression running amok often leads to the inconsiderate behavior that has become so prevalent these days.

One might question if it's really acceptable to text at the dinner table while ignoring those around you. And what about interrupting, disregarding, or needlessly embarrassing others? Especially annoying are children in restaurants whose parents have failed to teach them table manners. From screeching while jumping up and down in their booth to eating spaghetti with their fingers, a chaotic scene is inadvertently created for neighboring diners. I believe children who lack acceptable manners should eat at home—or better yet, in solitary confinement—until they become civilized. Politeness also counts, and to be a nicer person you must show respect and kindness to others—yes, even to those who may not deserve it.

Some claim you can actually be *too* nice. They say people may interpret being overly nice as a sign of weakness, or perhaps they consider a too-nice person a patsy, a pushover, or a total sucker. Others may become suspicious of one's motive. "Why is this guy being so decent? What does he really want? Better keep a hand on my wallet."

The disregard of others is often traced directly to an overly permissive upbringing. For example, children are often put in a position of authority by being consulted about matters better left to adults. It's okay to ask what a child wants for dinner, but does it benefit the family when every dinner must be pepperoni pizza, chicken fingers, or a tantrum? And if the family vacation was planned for a trip to the Grand Canyon, is it wise to change the venue to Disneyland because your unreasonable child is having a total meltdown?

Some parents believe that indulging a child's every whim is a measure of their love for them; and these are the ones who just can't say "no". Sorry folks, you've got that all wrong. The very best parents say "no" often, and that's how children learn to cross streets, avoid hot stoves, and get along with others. Without such restrictions children would be dashing into traffic, ending up in burn wards, and making lifelong enemies. Is that really preferable to saying "no" when appropriate?

Children need to know that some things in life are uncomfortable; that's how they learn to cope. They also must know that some things are worth waiting for, because instant gratification often leads to selfish, entitled, and narcissistic personalities. Kids should understand that parents are in charge, and parents should realize they are parents, not best friends. Don't worry, if you're a parent who often says "no" your kids will probably love you even more, because they will recognize that you genuinely care.

Society's primary need is for people to get along with others, because without positive relationships there would be isolation, loneliness, and widespread unhappiness. Nevertheless, people are often nasty, mean, and alienate others for no apparent reason. They may act that way in order to feel better about themselves, but how about the feelings of everyone else? Nasty people disrupt social relationships; they are manipulative, judgmental, insulting, and no doubt about it, a giant pain in the neck. We've probably all known people like that–but not for long.

At the extreme end of "nasty" are hate groups. A hate group is a social group that advocates hostility toward members of a race, religion, gender, sexual orientation, ethnicity, or any other sector of society that differs from themselves. But why the hate? How can anyone hate every single member a certain race without knowing even one of them? That's not only illogical; it's certifiably crazy.

In the show *"South Pacific"* by Rogers and Hammerstein, there is a song that explains much of what causes such hate.

You've got to be taught before it's too late,
Before you are six or seven or eight,
To hate all the people your relatives hate,
You've got to be carefully taught!

Persuasive leaders who appeal to people's fears, and dissatisfactions may also provoke hatred toward those considered responsible for their unhappiness. For example, prior to World War II Adolph Hitler and Benito Mussolini were fascist dictators who promised discontented followers a return to the glorious days of the past, while blaming their countries' problems on the ravages of capitalism and socialism. Even our current president took a page out of the same book and promised to "make America great again", while provoking hostility toward the former administration, corrupt media, and every human being on earth who opposed him.

It is difficult to understand those drawn to the Ku Klux Klan. This reactionary movement was founded shortly after the Civil War by extremists who believed in white supremacy, nationalism, anti-Semitism, and anti-Catholicism; or in their own words, the "purification" of American society. They dress in white sheets and silly conical hats as if they're off on a Halloween jaunt, but over the years they've caused great fear and incalculable damage to society.

Especially baffling is why any sane person would care to become a neo-Nazi. That sad group seeks to revive the ideology of Nazism, with beliefs in ultra nationalism, xenophobia, homophobia, and anti-Semitism. Holocaust denial is a common feature, as is the "heil" sign, and overuse of Nazi swastikas. Like KKK members, neo-Nazis have short memories; they fail to understand why their attitudes and values during past years were overwhelmingly rejected. Amazingly, they don't even recall the punishing defeats they suffered.

I once met a young person who claimed to be a neo-Nazi. I began by asking, "What's with the anti-Semitism? Have you ever actually met a Jewish person?"

"I don't have to; I know they're all the same. They're mostly wealthy capitalists; and they control the government, the banks, and the media. They're also stingy, greedy, and worst of all, they don't believe in Christ."

"Are you aware that Jesus was Jewish?"

"You're making that up."

"No, really, check it out on Google. He was born Jewish and he died Jewish. Just one more question; what goes on at your meetings? I mean, do you just stand around and say 'Heil Hitler' every so often?"

"Don't be silly. We have speakers, some entertainment, and maybe tell a few jokes."

"Jokes? What do neo-Nazis find so funny?"

"Mostly jokes about the Holocaust hoax, or about communists or cheap Jews."

"How about refreshments? Do you serve coffee and doughnuts, for example?"

"Sometimes we do," he answered, "but I happen to hate coffee."

"As much as Jews?"

"It's a toss-up."

Neo-Nazis and the KKK are just two of the hate groups that exist in America. According to those who track such groups, there are more than 900 organizations that regularly disparage an entire class of people. Most groups are located in the southern part of the country, but a few exist almost everywhere else. Unable to defend their views on the basis of logic or common sense, some groups now claim to offer what they call "alternative viewpoints". But calling bigotry, fascism, and irrational hatred a "viewpoint" is like calling a suicide bomber "rude".

Most Americans don't believe in extremism, except the wacky few unable to control their animosity. There is enough hatred in this world, actually, too much; so when it comes to nice vs. nasty, nice seems so much easier and more sensible. Finally, you have to remember that "nice" brings pleasure, satisfaction, and joy, whereas "nasty" results in disagreement, cruelty, and spitefulness. Your choice should be as clear as a cloudless sky.

Health

One of the most common greetings among friends is "Hi, how are you?" The meaning of that question assumes one cares about the health of the person being greeted, but that's not necessarily the case. The answer is supposed to be, "Fine, thanks," or possibly "Good–and you?" On the other hand, the person you're addressing might say, "Well, now that you ask…" Whoops! Hold it right there; that's not right. You really don't want to know about someone's recent troubles or afflictions. The person is supposed to stick to the script. When someone asks how you are, "Fine" is the only acceptable answer. Any further elaboration can only annoy, strain the relationship, or prompt you to glance at your watch and say something rude, like "Sorry, I've got to be going."

We generally assume people are in good health unless they show up in a wheel chair or on crutches. It wasn't always that way, largely because modern medicine has eliminated many conditions that previously plagued the general population. If one sneezed a century ago, which was a common sign of worse things to come, it was assumed he or she was ready to give up the ghost. So they would say "Gesundheit!" which was German for "good health", while implying regret for an obvious deteriorating condition. Later, people said, "Bless you!" or among the more religious, "God bless you!" These days, when people hear a sneeze they often say nothing, other than the occasional, "You might want to wipe that stuff off your lapel."

The subject of health considers the state of one's physical, mental, and social well-being. Individual health depends on lifestyle, over which you have some control; environment, over which you have less control;

and your genetic makeup inherited from your parents, over which you have no control. So if you were born with a predisposition to any number of unpleasant conditions, blame your parents. Don't worry—they're used to it.

Everyone realizes from an early age that some day they will die. Yes, death may be a depressing fact of life, but sadly, no one can escape that fate. The trick is to push that ominous moment as far into the future as possible, and that's where good health comes in. One is advised to embrace a healthy diet, avoid gaining weight, stay active, and sleep seven or eight hours a night. The healthiest people are usually those with sufficient incomes, a higher education, satisfactory social life, and reasonable coping skills. These types also have a better chance of avoiding mental illness, eating disorders, and depression. My guess is they're probably better looking, as well.

On the other hand, if your life is truly miserable and you feel there is little to live for, you're advised to smoke, overeat, hit the bottle regularly, abuse drugs, avoid exercise, get little sleep, and ignore medical professionals who offer advice.

Like most areas of life, good fortune goes a long way in promoting good health. Some at the age of ninety have never had a broken bone, while a three-year-old kid can slip on a banana peel and end up in a plaster cast. That's mostly a matter of luck. Of course, luck can be tempered by living a more careful life, like always crossing with the light, obeying the speed limit, and avoiding run-ins with deranged drivers.

The medical profession has done a remarkable job of caring for us. Since 1900 the life expectancy of Americans has increased by thirty years, the last six of which were added since 1990. Those improvements were fostered by greater access and affordability of health care, advances in pharmaceutical developments, improved medical training, and more attention paid to preventative measures.

As to pharmaceutical developments, have you noticed the recent surge of TV advertising for prescription drugs? Cialis, Eliquis, Lyrica, Humera and Celebrex are a few of the top ten that have recently jam-packed the airways with commercials. Pharmaceutical companies spent nearly five billion in advertising dollars during the past year promoting their products. I personally find these messages annoying, especially the alleged lovers sitting in separate bathtubs. Worse yet is the small print describing possible side effects, such as sudden loss of hearing or vision, dizziness, and almost everything else between an upset stomach and congestive heart failure.

Every ad ends with the identical line: "Ask your doctor if ____ is right for you!" All you want to say is why don't *you* ask *your* doctor why he or she would prescribe any one of these treacherous products that litter TV and do little more than irritate viewers? And, by the way, why are prices for drugs soaring beyond the reach of those needing them to survive? The simple answer, I recently discovered, is because drug manufacturers' monopolies allow them to charge whatever they please. Prescription drug spending in the U.S. now exceeds that in all other countries of the world, and sadly, the situation is unlikely to change. Your only recourse, it seems, is to stay healthy or take another Advil and forget about it.

Improved medical progress has been a blessing for most, but it has done little for hopeless hypochondriacs. If you've never had the opportunity of knowing a hypochondriac, your life has been lacking unique and incomparable drama. Hypochondriacs worry constantly about having a serious illness, despite the absence of any genuine medical evidence. They become unduly alarmed about symptoms they detect, although the symptoms may be insignificant. Even after a complete medical examination and being assured there is nothing to worry about, hypochondriacs often express skepticism of the doctor's diagnosis. With a hypochondriac a sneeze is never just a sneeze. It could be a cold, the flu, or maybe something incredibly bizarre that medical science has yet to identify. Fortunately, having an anxiety disorder is rarely fatal.

A genuine mental illness is a disease that causes disturbances in thought or behavior, resulting in an inability to cope with life's ordinary demands. It's estimated that roughly a quarter of all adults suffer from some form of mental illness, which has now become the leading cause of disability in this country. We used to say, "Ignore him, he's just a bit cuckoo, or maybe he has a few screws loose". But today it's more specific, as the more than 200 forms of mental illness include dementia, depression, bipolar disorder, schizophrenia, and endless anxiety disorders. Symptoms may include changes in mood or personality, and odd social habits, such as carrying on lengthy conversations with yourself loud enough to be heard a block away. Mental health problems may be related to excessive stress, dramatic events, genetic factors, biochemical imbalances, or a combination of these.

According to the World Health Organization, good mental health as "a state of well-being in which the individual realizes his or her own abilities, can cope with the normal stresses of life, works productively, and is able to make a contribution to the community". In many cases, that's easier said than done. Teens, especially, often suffer mental health issues in response to social pressures. Teen-age issues include depression, eating disorders, and drug abuse. With proper care and treatment many afflicted individuals learn to cope or recover from emotional disorders. That being said, we all know a few who continue to walk around in a perpetual haze. Many of them may be relatives or close friends that we think of as "eccentric".

Choosing a medical professional is as risky as choosing a defense attorney when accused of a serious felony. You have little to go on but the person's reputation or a recommendation from a trusted friend. In some cases the doctor is assigned to you and you have little to say about it. But when there is a choice you should check out the basic details on his or her website and then have a chat to determine your compatibility. Is the doctor easy to talk to? I personally like a doctor who displays a friendly smile. How about the office? Is it neat and clean? Erma Bombeck warns, *"Never go to a doctor whose office plants have died."*

While doctors are better trained and more knowledgeable than ever, they are still unable to perform the magical cures many patients expect. Still, good medical care usually lessens physical pain, which Saint Augustine claimed centuries ago to be *"the greatest of all evils"*.

I met my first doctor, Doctor Bill, on a tennis court during a doubles match many years ago. Having twisted an ankle, the good doctor suggested I go to his office, which was about a block from the tennis court. I hobbled over, he applied some ice, wrapped the ankle, and we became good friends; yes, even before he refused to send a bill.

What struck me about Doctor Bill was his calm professionalism and keen sense of humor. He smiled a lot and was always at ease. Though our tennis rarely improved, our relationship grew closer as the years passed. I generally required little medical treatment, but I never missed an annual exam.

I recall two important pieces of advice, which I pass on to you at no additional cost. "First," he said, "as you get older you will have slight pains, assorted aches, and unfamiliar twinges. Ignore them all. They will disappear within a week or two, and if they don't, call me." The second piece of advice is, "Avoid all pharmaceuticals, including vitamins. Of course, you should take antibiotics for infections and something for a bad headache, but skip all the other stuff. As for vitamins, a well balanced diet will provide all the vitamins and minerals you need. Besides, most of what's in those pills is peed away to no one's benefit other than the pill company."

Doctor Bill died several years ago, at a ripe old age, and it's a loss that still affects me. At his memorial service I spoke to his daughter. I knew Bill did not treat her, but I assumed he recommended the doctor who did. I got the name of her doctor and saw him for the next two years.

One day the new doctor arranged a heart scan by a technician who visited the office once each week. My appointment was scheduled for ten o'clock and—as is my habit—I arrived five minutes early. At ten thirty I was still in the waiting room. When I spoke to the receptionist, she assured me the technician was with another patient and would be available "any minute". I received the same response twenty minutes later, only this time with some obvious annoyance. Ten minutes later I suggested we reschedule the appointment, because I had another meeting elsewhere. She sneered at my request; yes, it was definitely a sneer. I said goodbye and left. The next day the doctor informed me I was no longer his patient. I was being fired! Fired for what? Defiance? Insubordination? Mutiny? I could not have been more polite, but who knows what story the unhappy receptionist told the doctor?

That's Life

Which brings me to my current doctor, a pleasant man more in the manner of Doctor Bill, who so far has never kept me waiting more than five minutes. So what's with doctors who totally disregard a patient's time? Is it poor scheduling, greed, arrogance? I can only suggest that doctors who keep patients waiting for hours are rude and lack all regard for patients on whose loyalty their livelihood depends. I once suggested to a dentist that he consider taking on fewer patients, because there were invariably emergencies, late arrivals, and numerous crises that forced patients to wait endlessly. "If by taking on fewer patients you end up with extra time on your hands," I proposed, "have a cup of coffee or take a walk around the block." He looked at me as though my space ship had just landed outside the office door.

Like most doctors, my new one generally errs on the side of caution. Several tests are suggested, "just to be certain". I reject most recommendations, not because I think I know more than the expert, but because I alone know how I feel. Additional tests can always be performed, but one must trust one's feelings and avoid being intimidated into an endless series of tests to accommodate unfounded medical suspicions, or perhaps keep the doctor bulletproof from potential legal action.

Sam Goldwyn once said, *"A hospital is no place to be sick"*. How right he was. I once spent a miserable night in a hospital because I had played tennis, became dehydrated, drank a martini, and passed out. I was otherwise in fine shape. I arrived by ambulance and was immediately put into intensive care and attached to several monitors, with tubes and wires emanating from every body part. Within an hour I was conscious and being interrogated as if I had just robbed a jewelry store.

I had virtually no sleep that night, because it seemed that every fifteen minutes there was a nurse checking or administering one thing or another. At three in the morning I called my wife and requested she pick me up. I was checking out. "You can't do that!" said the nurse. "Your doctor has not released you." I told her I was releasing myself, and proceeded to disconnect every tube and wire previously attached. Sometimes, perhaps not often, but sometimes the patient knows best.

Also, as Hippocrates, the great ancient Greek physician once said, *"There are times when doing nothing is also a good remedy."*

And speaking of Hippocrates, he also said, *"Health is the greatest of human blessings"*. Now who's going to argue with an ancient Greek genius?

Investing

Investing generally means putting money to use in some way that offers a profitable return. It also means devoting time and energy to a particular undertaking with the expectation of a worthwhile result; for example, teaching your daughter that kicking her older brother in the shins is unacceptable behavior. The entire family benefits from time invested in that pursuit, especially your son with the battered shins.

Benjamin Franklin had yet another investment in mind when he said, *"An investment in knowledge pays the best interest"*. In other words, Ben suggests you invest in yourself by becoming educated. Though higher education these days is costlier than ever, Derek Bok, former president of Harvard University, advises, *"If you think education is expensive, try ignorance"*.

The Bureau of Labor Statistics reports that those with a Master's Degree have an income three times higher than those with a high school diploma. And the unemployment figure for high school graduates is double that of those holding college degrees. If that doesn't convince you that investing in knowledge is a good bet, maybe you should consider becoming a rock star, try out for an NBA basketball team, or wait for a wealthy relative to die. But don't hold your breath waiting for any of *that* to happen.

Every investment, like life itself, involves risk, and before jumping in you should determine what level of risk feels comfortable. For example, driving while drunk is one of the most foolish risks one can take, because it can result in a smashed car, if not serious injury or death to you or someone else. If, on the other hand, you buy a two-dollar

Powerball lottery ticket, you can—and probably will—lose only two dollars. Incidentally, among high-risk activities, winning the Powerball jackpot is the height of improbability. In fact, you're much more likely to be attacked by a shark, die from a bolt of lightning, or get crushed beneath a vending machine. Yes, having one of those immense snack dispensers fall on you is far more probable than you winning a jackpot. And that's about as hopeless as odds get.

Every financial investment requires money, and for some that's the main problem.

Many people are simply unable to save. Those with insufficient incomes spend every penny to feed and shelter themselves, with nothing left over. Others spend more than they earn, and that situation is encouraged by the ease with which you can borrow money on a credit card. So if you find yourself short a few hundred dollars at the end of the month, why worry? Just put it on your card.

"Why not simply stop spending?" asks the voice in your head.

"Mind your own business," you answer; "I'll pay it off next month."

But you don't—because you lack self-control, have little guilt about going into debt, and are totally devoid of any investment knowledge. If you are among those who lack the discipline to save money, don't give up; it is possible to change your habits, see the light, and join the happy association of successful investors.

The purpose of all investments is to generate additional money for future use. Your goal should be to produce enough income by the time you retire to live comfortably without your normal paycheck. So how much will you need, you may ask? The Government Accountability Office suggests that one can retire comfortably with a nest egg of between one and two million dollars. And how much have people actually saved? One third have no retirement funds at all. None! Nada! Zip! And the typical family savings these days is about $63,000. Obviously there's a problem, but not one that is necessarily insurmountable.

One solution—perhaps not the best—may be to keep working until you fall off your chair one day and simply expire beneath your desk. A more reasonable plan, however, would be to start saving and investing immediately, because the longer you wait the more uncomfortable your future will be. If, for example, you invested $5000 in a retirement account at the age of 35 and added $200 dollars a month until you reached the age of 65, assuming an annual rate of return of 8%, you would end up with about $334,000. But if you had begun investing at the age of 20, you would end up with $1,127,000. That is the magic of compound interest, and that is why you must begin to invest as soon as possible.

Investments come in all sizes and every degree of risk. The safest and perhaps easiest choice is to open an interest-bearing savings account at a bank or savings institution that is federally insured. Those accounts pay very little interest these days, which may not get you close enough to your goal, but they are preferable to burying a coffee can full of cash in the back yard. If you need a greater return on your investment you must consider riskier alternatives, and those may include government or corporate bonds, common stocks, real estate, and collectables, like coins, precious gems, antique autos, and fine art.

Each of those categories may provide healthy returns on your investments, but each requires you to select a specific item in which to invest, and that's when people often break out in hives over the decision. Stocks or bonds or both? A condo at the beach or a storefront downtown? An Andy Warhol lithograph or a portrait of a clown painted on velvet by the oddball in the apartment downstairs? Toss a coin, throw a dart, consult an astrologist, or pray for guidance? Relax; help is on its way.

You may be tempted to avoid making any decision and instead hire an investment expert. Professionals are paid a fee based on the value of your portfolio, or may charge for advice on an hourly basis. In any event, fees are higher than you think. For example, if the return on your investment is 8% per year, and the advisor fee is 1%, you are actually paying 12% for advice. No great bargain, when you consider it that way.

So what's an investor to do? My personal advice is to do it yourself and keep it simple. First, you should realize that no one, not even your genius advisor, is able to choose individual stocks or mutual funds that will consistently beat the market. Most advisors cannot even match the return of the Standard & Poor's 500 stock index. You, on the other hand, can purchase shares of Fidelity's S&P 500 Index Fund, which consists of all 500 stocks and charges a management fee of .035% per year. No fuss, no sweat, and you'll never do worse than the market, because the S&P 500 *is* the market.

You might also consider the strategy of the Small Dogs of the Dow. Here's how that works: Begin with the 30 companies in the Dow Jones Industrial Average; select the ten companies paying the highest dividends; now select the five of those that sell for the lowest price. Purchase an equal dollar amount of each of the five companies, hold for exactly one year, and rebalance at the end of the year as outlined above. It doesn't matter what the company does, what it's selling for, or even if it's profitable. You will outperform the major averages 85% of the time, and you will sleep in worry-free comfort.

If you are attracted to mutual funds, you should buy those that have appreciated the most in a reasonable time span. Most of this information is available on line and is easy to access. Funds that have appreciated the most are the ones that are likely to continue appreciating. Again, forget what stocks the fund holds. Buy what's going up and hold until they stop going up or other funds appear that are going up even more rapidly. This will take more time than the previous investment suggestions, but the time spent should be more profitable.

Real estate is a wonderful investment, but it takes time and is far more complicated than buying stocks and bonds. To begin you must locate an attractive property, generally get a mortgage covering much of the purchase price, and rent the place to a tenant. You will pay the mortgage, property taxes, and maintenance, all of which should be covered by the monthly rent with, hopefully, a small profit left over.

So what could go wrong? Oh, brother! Where to begin? There's the possibility you could go for several months without a tenant. You might lower the rent, but they're still staying away in droves. Finally you settle on a rental figure so low you must add funds each month just to stay afloat. There is also the slight risk that your carefully vetted tenant could damage the property beyond an amount covered by the security deposit. Yes, that does happen, and one rarely sees the devastation coming.

But wait, there's more. You've invested in this jewel of a property for a regular cash flow and growth of your equity, and you hope for a modest appreciation in the property's value, but none of those results is assured. And if real estate values go down, as they sometimes do, you may not be able to sell the property, except at a painful loss. Meanwhile, costs continue, you curse the day you became a real estate investor, and a good night's sleep will be as unattainable as your fantasy uncle from out of nowhere leaving you a massive fortune.

On the other hand, if everything goes right, you may have found the golden goose that will allow you to spend Christmas in Aspen or even fund a week-long jaunt to Paris.

About collectibles, collect what you love, despite what everyone else collects. The reason is that you may be living with your collection for years. If you have a passion for baseball cards, go for them. If you hate non-representational art, by all means avoid it. It doesn't matter what you collect—postcards, stamps, books, old photos, vinyl records, tea pots, matchbooks, even classic lunch pails will appeal to someone else sometime in the future. And when it's time to cash in your chips, if you can bring yourself to part with them, you will be rewarded, sometimes beyond your wildest dreams.

In conclusion, there are a number of guidelines that may be helpful on your safari through the investment jungle that lies ahead.

- *All investments are driven by the human emotions of fear and greed.*
- *Any stock or fund can do anything at any time without warning or reason.*
- *Markets will do whatever they must to confound the greatest number of investors.*
- *Just because an investment is doing poorly doesn't mean it can't do worse.*
- *No investment should keep you awake at night. Sell down to the sleeping point.*
- *When an investment sounds too good to be true, it generally is.*

The importance of investing is to provide a comfortable life when you are ready to stop working at your usual job. This might happen when you receive your first Social Security check, or even before that time. If you invest seriously and consistently, your income from investments will continue to grow and furnish an income that exceeds the one that supported you most of your life. That's the goal, and for some disciplined and fortunate people, that's also the happy reality.

Attitude

Attitude is the tendency to think, feel, or act in a certain way about people, ideas, or events. Attitudes may be conscious or unconscious, as well as positive, negative, or indifferent, as they guide our decisions and influence our behavior. For example, one's attitude about kissing on the first date may be "never", because that's what our strict parents taught us; "often", because it feels so good; or "it depends", because you may never see your first date again, or if you do, "the bloom may be off the rose", as they say.

Attitudes can be the result of your upbringing, experience, or prejudice, and they generally influence the way you conduct yourself. For a variety of reasons, attitudes over time may change. In 1994, for example, 80 percent approved the death penalty in the U.S. Today, 60 percent of Americans say they would choose an alternative punishment. The same goes for political preferences during election cycles. Those who are fed up with current politics vote to replace the scoundrels running things, and a different group is elected to clean up the mess left by the former group. However, the duration of *their* term could be no longer than a solar eclipse.

Attitudes may also change over time on the subjects of school prayer, marijuana, abortion, television violence, and almost every other headline-worthy debate. Attitudes change because with more experience, maturity, and observation, we may evaluate things differently.

Attitudes are also affected by one's personality; that is, whether you are an optimist or a pessimist. Do you see the glass as half full or half empty? The attitude of optimists is generally more productive; or as Winston Churchill once said, *"I am an optimist—it doesn't seem much use being anything else."* Some believe that one is born with optimistic or pessimistic tendencies. Thus, parents may say, "He was born a sourpuss and has become progressively gloomier as the years drag on." Or, "She was a cheerful angel at birth, and today, if anything, she's an even a greater bundle of joy."

But what does science say? Researchers agree that most babies are born optimists, though I can't imagine how that is determined. Do they smile more or kvetch less? New brain scan studies from Michigan State University indicate that certain attitudes may be hardwired in one's head, Thus, one may emerge at birth an optimist or pessimist, which creates another good reason to love your parents, or perhaps condemn them for passing on defective genes.

The phenomenon known as Murphy's Law is considered the defining attitude of pessimists. It is often misquoted as, *"Anything that can go wrong, will go wrong"*. That certainly sounds cynical, but Murphy's actual quote was somewhat different and not particularly pessimistic. Here's the real story:

Edward A. Murphy, Jr. was an engineer on the rocket-sled experiments performed by the U.S. Air Force in 1949. As the name implies, a rocket sled is a test platform, propelled by rockets, that slides along a set of rails. The purpose of the 1949 experiments was to test a person's physical tolerance to extreme acceleration. One test involved a set of 16 accelerometers mounted on different parts of the subject's body. There were two ways to glue each sensor to its mount, and somebody methodically installed all 16 the *wrong* way.

The engineer, Murphy, concluded that: *"If there are two or more ways to do something, and one of those ways can result in a catastrophe, someone will do it."*

In other words, Murphy's Law is actually a positive message. Not only is it a warning about what can go wrong, it also implies that if there were only *one* way to do something it would be almost impossible for the result to fail.

Within months, Murphy's Law spread to various technical cultures connected to aerospace engineering. Variants were developed somewhat later based on the proposition that *"Anything that can go wrong will go wrong"*. Following are a few of the popular corollaries to the original Law, all of which have become essential pessimistic dogma.

- *If there is a possibility of several things going wrong, the one that will cause the most damage will be the first to go wrong.*
- *Matter will be damaged in direct proportion to its value.*
- *If there is a worse time for something to go wrong, it will happen then.*
- *If everything seems to be going well, you have obviously overlooked something.*
- *If several things that could go wrong have not gone wrong, it would have been ultimately beneficial if they had gone wrong.*
- *If anything can't go wrong, it will anyway.*
- *It is impossible to make anything foolproof, because fools are so ingenious.*

There are endless variations on these corollaries, but you get the point; pessimists believe there are times when everything is bound to go against you, as if guided by the malicious hand of fate. A much earlier parody, attributed to James Payn from 1884, reinforces the pessimistic notion that if anything can go wrong, it will:

I never had a slice of bread, particularly large and wide,
That did not fall upon the floor, and always on the buttered side!

Getting back to the subject of attitude, the genes you inherit play a part in forming attitudes, but more important is the family environment one experiences during early childhood. A sense of belonging determines our degree of security in later life. Did your folks instill in you a sense of security and of being loved? Or did they act as though you were more an irritation than gift from heaven? Perhaps they made secret trips to the attic, where they marked months off a calendar until you reached the age of eighteen, at which time they planned to say a final *adios* as they changed the lock on the front door.

The role of one's parents is critical in the development of future attitudes. If you were reprimanded more than praised during those early years your attitude may be that nothing you do will ever turn out right. We all know people like that, and now you know why they're like that.

Having commendable parents is entirely beyond your control and simply a matter of luck. The two individuals (or sometimes one) who manage your upbringing were a fact of life months before you were born. You were not consulted, nor was it considered any of your business. So there they were, two strangers having been determined by accident or fate and little more logic than a coin toss. If you got good parents, be happy; and if they turned out to be mediocre, be happy they weren't worse.

My own good fortune was to have genuinely wonderful parents. It took a number of years for that realization to sink in, but compared to other parents I've seen, they were decent and caring people. Neither parent had more than an eighth-grade education, but both were knowledgeable about the way the world worked. Most importantly, they had a keen sense of humor, so getting through the Great Depression, for example, while no fun, was made tolerable by laughing at life. They could sing, dance, make jokes, and have an occasionally pleasant time raising their children.

Though my brother and I rarely got along, our parents treated quarrels with impartiality and fairness. Nevertheless, my early teen years were difficult, because nearly every teen is conflicted, to one degree or another, about almost everything. Teens want to be treated as adults, but they are usually ill equipped to behave that way. And so they often develop an "attitude" involving unattractive personality quirks, like arrogance, contempt, and disrespect. Such people invariably display a negative outlook, are generally uncommunicative, and frequently radiate unhappiness. Welcome to teen world.

One Saturday night when I was nearly fifteen years old, I was waiting to go out with friends. My father innocently asked where I was going, and for whatever reason I replied, "What's it to you?" I knew at once I had made a terrible mistake. Without a single word, my father slapped me in the face. In the face! He had never done such a thing in my entire life. He then said, "I'm you father; you don't have to like me, but you *do* have to show me respect!"

Attitude

The slap didn't really hurt, but his words brought tears to my eyes. As he left the room, I stood there crying for several minutes, wishing I could take back my words. The next morning I apologized. My father put an arm around me and said, "I owe you an apology, too. Parents are not supposed to lose control; it won't happen again. I hope you know that I love you." This drama took place dozens of years ago, but I recall every detail as though it were yesterday.

Having an attitude is a terrible burden. It's a common form of hostility designed to repel people. Perhaps you've had a restaurant waiter with an attitude who treated you as though he considered you more an irritation than a patron. At a recent dinner our waiter never once smiled, ignored us for half an hour before taking our order, served the wrong entrée, and was nowhere to be found when we needed a fork, and finally, our check. Perhaps he was waiting to hear from his agent that he scored an acting job, or that a publisher just purchased his manuscript. In the meantime, it seemed he was doing us a giant favor just speaking to us.

Extensive research at Stanford University reveals the following extraordinary statistic: Success is 87 percent the result of your attitude, while your skill, ability, and knowledge make up the other 13 percent. That alone should convince you to improve your attitude. Those with positive attitudes generally achieve commensurate rewards; but many successes would never have been achieved if those with positive attitudes had listened to their critics.

For example, Enrico Caruso, the world's greatest tenor, was told his voice "sounded like a tin can." Walt Disney was fired from the Kansas City Star in 1919 because, his editor said, he "lacked imagination and had no good ideas." Henry Ford was told to forget the car business, and Marie Curie was encouraged to drop her fixation on radioactivity. Friends told Laurence Olivier to abandon acting, and in Fred Astaire's first screen test, an executive wrote: "Can't sing, can't act, slightly balding, can dance a little." Benjamin Franklin was advised to stop fiddling with lightning. And finally, Christopher Columbus took fourteen years to raise funds for ships and crew before setting out on his explorations. Though the science and culture of the day said the world was flat, Queen Isabella and King Ferdinand had faith in the

Italian explorer. With faith and a positive attitude, Columbus took just six months to discover the New World.

So what can we learn from all this? Attitudes are an expression of who we are and what we believe. Even when non-verbal, such as a bumper sticker or a T-shirt message, your attitude is revealed for all to see. Consider the message sent by tattoos. Years ago a friend, in a moment of overwhelming passion, had tattooed on his forearm "June", the name of his current love. A month later, however, he and June were bitter enemies, and now he faced the painful process of removing the tattoo or getting stuck with her disagreeable name on his arm forever. In a creative flash that surprised even me, I suggested he add the number 14, and a small American flag, and claim that Flag Day, June 14th, expressed his love of country. Some may ask, what if her name had been Elizabeth? Sorry, the only recourse would be to search for another lovable Elizabeth, or face the pain and discomfort of the tattoo's removal.

Attitude is also a choice; what you currently believe is not necessarily chiseled in stone. The same influences that form attitudes can also change attitudes. People can modify their points of view after observing the behavior of others they admire, or by developing positive feelings for ideas or events formerly considered undesirable. For example, a woman who believes strongly in abstinence before marriage may wish to remain a virgin until her wedding night. But when her fiancé expresses his overwhelming love and sexual desire she may relent and forever after rejoice in her change of attitude.

Choosing an attitude is choosing the kind of life you wish to live. Most people aspire to be socially acceptable; they want to be positive, popular, and productive; yet some have negative attitudes that antagonize and irritate. Bad attitudes are often the product of adverse experiences that cause stress, fear, resentment, and anger. To change a harmful attitude takes courage, but ridding yourself of negative baggage can change your life in unimaginable ways.

No less an authority than Founding Father, Thomas Jefferson, once said," *Nothing can stop the man with the right mental attitude from achieving his goal, while nothing on earth can help the man with the wrong mental attitude."*

Listen to Tom, folks; lose your negative ways, and you've got a good shot at becoming the next life of the party.

Music

Here's something you might have suspected but didn't really know for sure. The lyrics of recent No.1 popular songs are rated at a third grade reading level. Think about that. Lyrics these days are aimed at the reading aptitude of an eight to nine-year-old! A study by Andrew Powell-Morse claims that lyrics from Beyoncé, Foo Fighters, Adele, Eminem, and others reveal just how dumbed down lyrics are for songs that currently dominate the Billboard charts. The study analyzed the reading levels for 225 songs that spent three or more weeks atop Billboard's Pop, Country, Rock, and Hip-Hop song charts. Whereas chart-toppers in 2005 rated near a fourth grade level, a decade later that average has fallen like a drunk who missed the first step going down the basement stairway. In five of the last ten years the reading level of a Billboard No.1 single has persistently trended downward.

Exhibit A (unedited) comes from Lady Gaga and is entitled "John Wayne".

It's like; I just love a cowboy you know
I'm just like, I just, I know, it's bad
But I'm just like
Can I just like, hang off the back of your horse?

In contrast, consider the following lines from the long-ago pen of Cole Porter:

There's an oh, such a hungry yearning, burning inside of me

And this torment won't be through
Till you let me spend my life making love to you
Day and Night, Night and Day

Clearly, one song makes romantic sense and the other is absolute gibberish. Lady Gaga is popular and most agree she has musical talent, but apparently she's in desperate need of a lyricist. Cole Porter, on the other hand was a poet and a rhyming genius. For example, from the show "Kiss Me Kate", as the recently married character, Petruchio, thumbs through his old address book, he sings:

In dear Milano, where are you, Momo,
Still selling your pictures of the Scriptures in the Duomo?
And lovely Lisa, where are you, Lisa?
You gave a new meaning to the leaning tower of Pisa.

The last line is typical Cole Porter—a double entendre with explicit risqué intent.

Lerner and Loewe wrote some of the most memorable Broadway shows such as "Gigi", "Brigadoon", and "Camelot". Perhaps their finest show, however, was "My Fair Lady". Compare the Alan Jay Lerner words with any lyrics written today. The scene is one in which Professor Henry Higgins explains why he remains unmarried.

Let a woman in your life and your serenity is through,
she'll redecorate your home, from the cellar to the dome,
and then go on to the enthralling fun of overhauling you...
I'd be equally as willing for a dentist to be drilling than to ever let a
woman in my life.

Lyrics are only part of the contrast between current songs and those from years past; older songs generally had a melody. Today's crop of songs have little more than a persistent drum beat. Can you whistle any tune from "The Book of Mormon"? Even a most highly awarded show like "Hamilton" has no memorable melody you can hum as you exit the theater. So, who needs melody, you may ask? Only those who buy Irving Berlin's description of a pretty girl: *"like a melody that haunts you night and day"*.

You get the point; popular songs today, in my opinion, are so clearly inferior to those of the past, endless shame and embarrassment should be surging throughout the entire musical industry. The reasons for inferior music should be obvious: In olden days there were actual songwriters, people who wrote sweet melodies and poetic others who wrote the words. A few, like Porter and Berlin wrote both music and lyrics, but most others worked as a team, like George and Ira Gershwin and Richard Rogers and Oscar Hammerstein, who wrote a score of hit Broadway shows, like "The Sound of Music", "Carousel", and "The King and I". Today, however, performers generally write their own songs, even though most of them know next to nothing about composition and even less about the power and subtleties of the language in which they're writing.

There are exceptions, of course, like Bob Dylan who won a Nobel Prize for literature. The committee's citation said, *"For having created new poetic expressions within the great American song tradition."* Following are some lyrics from his popular "Blowin' in The Wind" from 1960:

Yes, and how many times must a man look up, before he can see the sky?
Yes, and how many ears must one man have,
before he can hear people cry?
Yes, and how many deaths will it take till he
knows that too many people have died?
The answer, my friend, is blowin' in the wind,
the answer is blowin' in the wind

Music is the art of sound that expresses ideas and emotions through the elements of rhythm, melody, and harmony. All the world's people, including isolated tribal groups, developed some form of music at least 150,000 years ago. The first instrument was thought to be the human voice, which probably accompanied the rhythm of some Neanderthal hitting a rock against a tree. This actually brings to mind a few of today's entertainers who sound like they're still hitting rocks against trees. Later came development of the flute, carved from bone or ivory, and the first stringed instrument, a lyre, which appeared in classical Greece.

Many of those who want to make music today often begin with a guitar, or the smaller ukulele, and strum and hum along and think what great fun this is! In time they may imagine, "Hey, what d'ya know, I'm a musician! Look out world, here I come". That's when someone with better musical sense should take them aside and explain the facts of life.

The variety of music today absolutely boggles the mind. It encompasses Opera, Folk Music, Classical, Country, Dance Music, Easy Listening, Electronic Music, Hip Hop, Rap, Blues, Gospel, Jazz, Latin, Pop, R&B, Soul, and Rock, to name just a few genres. And whatever you want to hear has been recorded, packaged, and is available to purchase for your enjoyment.

It may not surprise you to know that one's choice of music reveals distinct personality traits, just as one's choice of dress often does. For many of us, our taste in music is an integral part of our identity; what we listen to is who we are. The songs of our youth still fill our heads with stray lyrics and infectious melodies, defining the way we understood the world from that time on.

The link between musical preferences and personality is so strong that a quick glance at one's record collection reveals a wealth of information about the owner. Music psychology scholar Adrian North, PhD, conducted a three-year study correlating the musical preferences and personality traits of more than 36,000 participants. Dr. North determined, for example, that lovers of the classics are creative, introverted, and enjoy high self-esteem. The study also found that students who appreciate Beethoven had a considerably higher average SAT score than those who favored hip-hop. Hip-hop fans, on the other hand, were found to be extroverted and energetic listeners.

So, you may ask, who really cares? Analyzing music to death may very well destroy whatever delight a melody conveys. Are you any happier learning that Pop fans show a lack of creativity compared to other categories, or that Country listeners are unpretentious and empathetic. More to the point, if you like Bagpipe music and I prefer listening to Hungarian Rhapsody No. 2, does that mean we can never have lunch together? If the "twang" of Country music drives you up the wall, or if you would rather be water-boarded than forced to sit through a performance of *La Traviata*, does that spell the end of our relationship? Relax, there's plenty of room in the musical world for us all.

Music is the beauty and power of sound, and each of us can be thrilled or driven to tears by the way any given piece affects us. Though some consider a specific melody to be the equivalent of angels' voices, other may consider it noise, which is defined as "unwanted sound". Unfortunately, that's life.

Music communicates a feeling that no other medium can quite match. Consider for a moment what the popular film *Jaws* would have been without the John Williams' score, which ranks as some of the most terrifying music ever written for a movie. According to a 2005 survey by the American Film Institute, it remains among the top ten most memorable scores in movie history. Director Steven Spielberg compared Williams's score to Bernard Herrmann's equally frightening music in Alfred Hitchcock's *Psycho*. And *Casablanca*, often considered an absolute classic, would have been considerably less effective without the theme song, *As Time Goes By*.

Individual musical taste is very much like artistic taste; there is rarely a logical explanation for it. Why does one person love banjo music while another considers it a form of medieval torture? Some pay great amounts of money to attend a live performance of a Beethoven symphony, while others enjoy sleeping through it. So in addition to hearing complaints like, "You call that art?" one often hears, "You call that music?" As in most other such situations I say, "Each to his or her own bad taste"!

Many of my particular listening favorites come from what I consider the Golden Age of songwriting, the big band years. Almost anything written by George Gershwin, Irving Berlin, Harold Arlen, Jerome Kern, or Cole Porter can still express, by way of their unforgettable melodies, original, sensitive, and absolutely magical illusions. Many old tunes may pop into my head at any time, and I have no idea why. And every so often, the lyrics as well, such as *Love is Just Around the Corner* by Leo Robin, which is currently stuck between my ears.

> *Venus de Milo was noted for her charms,*
> *But strictly between us you're cuter than Venus,*
> *And what's more you've got arms.*

Though I know little about music, like many others, I remember what I've enjoyed in the past. For example, the first opera I ever saw was Puccini's *Madama Butterfly*, performed by the San Francisco Opera. I had read the libretto, so knew the general plot. But I was totally unprepared for one of the most beautiful musical experiences one can imagine. If you were not sobbing when the final curtain came down, you were obviously in a coma. On another occasion I attended a performance of the U.S. Marine Band. Established by an act of Congress in 1798, it is the oldest professional musical organization in the United States. When hearing seventy-five musicians play John Philip Sousa's *Stars and Stripes Forever*, it is impossible to stop your toe from tapping. In fact you want to leap up and march in time around the concert hall. It's infectious, irresistible and unforgettable!

Which leads me to a particular irritation known as *The Star-Spangled Banner*, the national anthem of our country. The lyrics come from a poem written in 1814 by amateur poet, Francis Scott Key, after he witnessed the bombardment of Fort McHenry by the Royal Navy during the War of 1812. The poem was set to the tune of a popular British song, renamed, and officially designated our national anthem 100 years later.

With its range of an octave and a half, our national anthem is nearly impossible to sing well. Many have tried, and most have failed. The anthem's other drawback is that it celebrates war. Is that really the proper model for a peace-loving nation?

And the rocket's red glare!
The bombs bursting in air!
Our anthem has been ridiculed for years, for example, what we sang

as children was: *"Oh say can you see any bed bugs on me? If you do, take a few; if you don't, nuts to you…*

Before 1931, other songs served as the American hymn, such as "My Country, 'Tis of Thee", as well as "America the Beautiful". Neither of those songs spoke of war or battles. But there's an even better solution out there waiting to replace our flawed anthem: Irving Berlin's "God Bless America".

God bless America, land that I love
Stand beside her and guide her
Through the night with the light from above

It's easy to sing, and its message is one all can embrace. I say let's ditch that Star Spangled nonsense and replace it with a decent, positive, and more beautiful anthem.

Tomorrow would not be soon enough.

Cruelty

Imagine walking into a room and seeing your child whirling around your pet kitten by its tail. Or perhaps he or she is tearing the wings off a butterfly or trying to set fire to the hamster. Better pay attention; there's trouble ahead. Cruelty to animals is not just a childish prank; it's a serious warning sign of later delinquency, violence, and criminal behavior. In fact, nearly every offender of a violent crime had a history of animal cruelty. Studies show that those who repeatedly torture small animals also have high levels of aggression toward people.

- Albert Desalvo, known as the "Boston Strangler", killed thirteen women, and admitted that as a child he shot arrows through the animals he trapped.
- Jeffrey Dahmer, nicknamed the "Milwaukee Cannibal", killed neighbors' pets as a child and later raped, murdered, and cannibalized seventeen men and boys.
- Ted Bundy watched his father torture small animals and grew up to outdo his Dad. He confessed to thirty homicides in seven states. And the list goes on.

Cruelty to animals is also considered a significant predictor of future domestic violence, because abusers target the powerless, which include spouses and children, as well as the elderly. The message is clear; you don't have to wait until your kid microwaves the pet rabbit to recognize you have a problem.

So why do children torture animals? Some simply don't realize that all living creatures experience pain and suffering. If parents discuss the similarities between animals and people, empathy may develop to prevent future cruelty. Another reason children are cruel to animals may be a result of having been abused themselves or living in an environment of domestic violence. Mistreated children often seek out their own victims, like a pet or sibling, in order to seek revenge.

Incidentally, just because you may have harmed an animal when you were a child does not mean you're about to become a serial killer. Perhaps you once kicked a dog in anger, and the guilt lingers. But it doesn't necessarily follow that swatting a pesky fly or spraying poison on termites chomping away at your foundation puts you in the same class as Vlad the Impaler.

Some consider the present-day practice of bullfighting the supreme example of animal abuse. Though legal in Spain, Mexico, and a few other countries, there are renewed calls to abandon the bloody tradition and reassess its place in today's culture. Proponents say bullfighting dates back thousands of years and represents a part of their cultural heritage, like for example, fiestas and flamenco dancing.

But animal rights groups maintain that bullfighting is never a fair fight. They say it's unthinkable that in the 21st century a spectacle that mistreats and kills an animal is considered a cultural event. Bullfighting is barbaric, they claim. How can crowds of people pay money and take pleasure in watching one lone creature–who's never done them any harm–get hacked to death? How can anyone with any compassion cheer and shout *"ole"* as lances and *bandarillos* are thrust into the animal's pain-wracked body?

My own experience many years ago resulted in conflicting emotions. A friend and I were at the Plaza de Toros de Las Ventas, the famous bullring in Madrid. The Plaza has a seating capacity of 25,000, and there wasn't an empty seat. While musicians played, an opening parade of matadors and supporting cast of bullfighters strutted around the ring before cheering fans. The participants took their places, and the first bull was released into the ring. But this was no ordinary bull. The monstrous black animal, weighing more than half a ton, galloped at full speed across the arena and made a spectacular leap over the fence and into the shocked front-row crowd. Patrons scattered as the team led the enraged beast back into the arena.

Out came the *picadors* on padded horses, but the bull made the initial move. He charged the first rider, lodged his horns beneath the horse's padding, and threw horse and rider to the ground. The crowd gasped in horror as the horse lay mortally wounded and the rider fled for his life. Next came the *banderilleros* with their barbed sticks. On the first pass the bull hooked an arm, and the wounded fighter raced to the protective wall spurting blood all the way. It was at this unforeseen moment I began to root for the bull.

Finally, the *matador* appeared in his glorious suit of lights. He carried a small red cape and a sword. After taunting the bull with several deft moves the crowd cheered wildly with one "*ole*" after another. Just when it appeared the fight was nearly over, the enraged bull charged and hooked the fighter in the groin and threw him over his head. He landed in a heap, fifteen feet away, and as others tried to distract the bull, the animal continued to stomp the motionless body.

Another matador soon appeared, and as he finally plunged his sword into the exhausted bull, the animal fell to the ground. The carcass was pulled out of the arena by a team of mules, and my friend and I left the field of battle as well. Watching further slaughter was out of the question. Yes, it was exciting and unconventional, but it was also cruel, barbaric, and I believe, no longer appropriate entertainment in a civilized world.

Cruelty is defined as the deliberate and malicious infliction of mental or physical pain upon persons or animals; and it is as old as the story of Cain killing his brother Abel. Though most people in the world have a sense of compassion, and are distressed when seeing others in harms way, occasionally you'll meet someone totally unaffected. That person may be rude or mean and have moments of cruelty or outbursts of rage. Where does this come from? Essentially, these are unhappy people, often with low self-esteem and an abundance of unresolved anger. When people like this become powerful leaders there are often reigns of terror that include genocide, inquisitions, executions, and sadistic torture.

Speaking of torture, it would be interesting to know about the people who invented the instruments that have produced such diabolical pain. They must have known their inventions created inconceivable agony. Were they at all concerned? Consider crucifixion, for example, or being boiled in oil, the guillotine, thumbscrews, being blinded, drawn and quartered, or the various methods of impalement. These were meant not only to kill, but also to make the victim suffer unimaginable pain. What kind of people condoned these practices? One can only guess it was a small, unhappy group operating, while everyone else looked the other way.

From the beginning of time enemies have been considered less than human. Thus, the perpetrator was not torturing another human, but something considered less than that. Studies show the psychological conflict of killing another human in cold blood, or inflicting torture on them. To overcome these natural inhibitions one must dehumanize the victim by considering them animals or dangerous predators. Dehumanization opens the door for cruelty and genocide. Throughout history slave owners considered slaves subhuman animals. American Indians were considered savages, Hutus in the Rwanda genocide called Tutsis cockroaches, and Nazis during the Holocaust referred to Jews as rats.

The Second World War is considered the single most destructive event in human history. More than seventy million people died in the war, most of them civilians. Many died in combat, but millions more were burned alive by incendiary bombs and, in the end, nuclear weapons. Worse yet were victims of genocide, and it was dehumanization that made that carnage possible.

The 1946 Nuremberg doctors' trial was the first of twelve military tribunals held in Germany after the war. The trial included twenty doctors and three administrators who stood accused of war crimes and crimes against humanity. They had participated in Hitler's euthanasia program, in which around 200,000 mentally and physically handicapped people—deemed unfit to live—were gassed to death. The defendants were charged with atrocities committed in the name of medical science, and the thousands of victims who suffered fiendish medical experiments included Jews, Roma, and Russians.

Some of these human guinea pigs were deprived of oxygen to simulate high altitude parachute jumps. Others were frozen, infested with malaria, or exposed to mustard gas. Doctors made incisions in their flesh to simulate wounds and introduced bacteria to induce gangrene. Some were made to drink seawater; others infected with typhus and other deadly diseases, or poisoned and burned with phosphorus. All the while medical personnel carefully recorded their agonized screams and violent convulsions.

What enables one group of people to treat another group as though they are less than human? The Nazis were frank about the status of their victims. They were subhuman and as such were excluded from the moral system that unites the human race. It's wrong to kill a person, but permissible to exterminate a rat. To the Nazis, the Jews, Gypsies and others were rats– dangerous, disease-carrying rats.

Among the wide-ranging activities of mankind there is nothing more purposefully cruel than war. War is a violent conflict between people of differing ideologies, during which scores of innocent people are killed– civilians as well as soldiers. And though one side may ultimately claim victory, both sides suffer immense damage and financial loss. William Tecumseh Sherman, the great Civil War General, said, *"War is Hell. It is cruelty, and you cannot refine it; and those who bring war to our country deserve all the curses and maledictions a people can pour out."* Let us hope current and future Congress members heed General Sherman's words.

The persistent threat these days of nuclear annihilation by some countries absolutely defies rationality. Do demented leaders, as well as American extremists, realize they are flirting with the end of civilization? A nuclear holocaust would completely devastate our rare planet, while relinquishing it to the only probable survivors–cockroaches, fruit flies, and amoebas. What kind of international dispute is worth contemplating that kind of horror?

Most Americans think of us as a "Peace-Loving Nation", but that is a myth that could not be further from the truth. A glance at history reveals that America has either been involved in armed conflict or conducted military operations over 90 per cent of the time we've existed as a nation. Just think about that! Whatever we may be, we are definitely not peaceful. The government invariably invokes national security when launching a war, but national security is rarely the reason. What danger did countries like the Philippines, Honduras, Vietnam or Iraq ever present to the American people? Almost every foreign war was initiated against countries that posed no direct threat to the United States. The notable exception was the war with Japan, declared after the bombing of Pearl Harbor. Shortly after the end of World War II the original War Department became the U.S. Department of Defense. Some would say that the former title was more descriptive and honest, but for public relations, the new name sounded less active and more reactive.

Americans are not essentially a cruel people, but neither are we, by any means, the nicest people on earth. There is a growing contempt on the part of certain Americans for those caught in the web of misfortune, dependency, and deprivation. Fellow citizens often disparage the poor, refer to the homeless as lazy, blame Blacks for the criminal culture, attribute obesity to the proliferation of food stamps, and consider all immigrants a deadly threat. To make matters worse, there is a growing lack of respect for other views and a nearly complete absence of civil conversation.

Violence, as well, has become more acceptable in our culture. Movies, for example, have become increasingly graphic, with the blood-spattered wall almost a cliché. There are also more violent video games, with scores based on the increased number of "kills". Our most popular sport is American football, where violent tackles are wildly applauded, while the players involved often develop brain damage. No less violent are hockey games and martial arts bouts, where contestants emerge looking like survivors of a car wreck. When so much violence surrounds us, why is anyone surprised that acts of bullying in schools and incidents of domestic violence are on the rise?

Rodney King, a Black citizen of Los Angeles was violently beaten while being arrested in 1992 by four police officers. A bystander videotaped the event, and the incident raised a public outcry among those who believed it was a racially motivated attack. The acquittal of the four defendants, charged with using excessive force, provided the spark that led to the Watts Riots. A few days into the uprising King publicly asked, *"Can we all get along? Can we stop making it horrible for the older people and the kids? ... It's just not right. It's not going to change anything. I mean, we're all stuck here for a while. Let's try to work it out."*

Years ago people seemed to be nicer to one another. View old movie from the forties or fifties and you will see acts of decency portrayed in "The Best Years of Our Lives" and "It's a Wonderful Life". Every movie was suitable for family viewing, cruelty never appeared, and even today, these iconic movies remain immensely entertaining. Not everything was better back then, but people, it seems, certainly were. Perhaps if we all tried a bit harder we could "try to work it out" and actually find a way to "all get along".

Humor

What's so funny? That's what everybody wants to know. Some people laugh at a joke; others groan. Great minds have been trying for years to plumb the depths of humor. Sigmund Freud suggested that humor allows us to express forbidden thoughts. Dirty jokes, for example, break the rules of society and provide guilty pleasure. Dark humor also provides similar satisfaction.

A man awakens from a two-week-long coma. As his wife changes out of the black clothes she's recently been wearing she says, "I just can't depend on you, can I?"

Humor enables us to cope with the challenges of life and laugh at the absurdities we face every day. It puts our fears in perspective so we can laugh away our troubles. The German philosopher, Immanuel Kant proposed that, *"Humor arises when we're presented with bizarre or startling information that is resolved unexpectedly."*

"I found my first gray pubic hair today and boy, was I thrilled, but not nearly as excited as the others in the elevator."

Comic humor, like a person slipping on a banana peel, makes us laugh at the ineptitude of others. As Mark Twain said, *"What's funny is when something bad happens to somebody else."* And it's even funnier when humor becomes bigoted and disparaging, as in the following examples of: 1. Parodies, 2. Polish jokes, and 3. Dumb-Blond jokes.

That's Life

1. *Jack was nimble and Jack was quick. One day he jumped over a candlestick.*
   His pants caught fire, Jack rose higher, and now he resides in a heavenly choir.
2. *How can we be sure Jesus was not born in Poland?*
   Obviously, they couldn't find three wise men or a virgin.
3. *A fellow bought his blond girlfriend a new cell phone. The following day he called to ask how the phone was working. "Just fine," she said, "but how did you know I was at Wal-Mart?"*

Humor, and its byproduct laughter, can also be healing. Some years ago Norman Cousins, the editor of the Saturday Review, contracted a rare disease and was given a few months to live. He took a sabbatical from work, checked into a hotel, and proceeded to watch humorous films, including old Marx Brothers movies and television comedies. Within six months his doctor proclaimed he was miraculously cured. It was no miracle, however, it was simply laughing until your stomach hurt. It has been shown that laughing decreases stress hormones, reduces pain, and aids in the healing process. As a happy bonus, laughter has no negative side effects. Norman Cousins died in 1990, exactly twenty-six years after he was advised by his doctor to get his affairs in order.

There are many kinds of humor, various categories of jokes, and an endless stream of sophisticated analyses of the entire subject; but scrutinizing humor to death may be counterproductive. As E.B. White said, *"Analyzing humor is like dissecting a frog. Few people are interested, and the frog dies of it."*

Most people believe they have a keen sense of humor when, in fact, many do not. However, a sense of humor is highly appreciated and considered important in attracting other people. It is one of the most critical characteristics in seeking a romantic partner—rated higher than wealth and good looks. How can you not love the person who makes you laugh and brightens your day with a silly joke?

The first joke I ever learned was a knock-knock joke. They were all the rage in those days, especially among four-year-olds. The joke went like this:

Humor

Knock-knock. - Who's there? - Hatch. - Hatch who? - Gesundheit!

Not exactly a thigh-slapper, but at four years of age I wasn't all that discerning, nor was I eyeing a career in comedy. The joke amused my friends, but irritated my brother, who was two years older and apparently more discriminating. He preferred jokes that were scatological–anything that included a private body part.

"If you tell that stupid joke one more time," he said, "I'm going to throw something!"

"I'm not telling that joke anymore," I answered. "I've got a better one; want to hear it?" After a long silence I said, "Well, anyway, here goes."

"Knock-knock."
"Who's there?" he reluctantly asked.
"Panther." Another long silence.
"Panther? Seriously?" Now he sounded intrigued. *"Panther who?"*
"Panther no panth, I'm going thwimming."

Then he threw a book at me that missed; but he barely restrained a giggle.

Since those early knock-knock days I've loved hearing, as well as telling jokes. I've also enjoyed reading about jokes and learning what makes a joke funny. As far as I'm concerned it's a simple matter; if it makes you laugh it's funny. Everyone's idea of funny is different and impossible to predict. But the best jokes appeal to almost everyone with a sense of humor. How can you not laugh at the Marx Brother's crowded cabin scene in "Night at the Opera", Woody Allen robbing a bank in "Take the Money and Run", or the campfire scene in Mel Brooks' "Blazing Saddles'? Those are hilarious moments that can bring tears of joy to the most cynical eyes.

The oldest jokes on record go back thousands of years, but sad to say, they're not very funny today. For example, consider this Greek joke from the 4th century:

That's Life

An unhappy old man attends the burial of his wife. When someone asks, "Who rests in peace here?" the old man answers, "Me, now that I'm rid of her."

Henny Youngman did it better with his one-liner, *"Take my wife... please."*

Youngman was the absolute king of one-liners. Following are a few of his best:

- *I've loved the same woman for 41 years. If my wife finds out, she'll kill me.*
- *When I read about the evils of drinking I gave up reading.*
- *The secret to a happy marriage remains a secret.*

Puns have been called the lowest form of humor. A pun is a joke exploiting the different possible meanings of a word or using words that sound alike but have different meanings. Some people think puns are the height of hilarity, while others moan and groan at the thought. You be the judge.

- *I'm reading a book about antigravity. It's impossible to put down.*
- *Those who prefer cremation to traditional burial are thinking outside the box.*
- *Sleeping is so natural to me I can do it with my eyes closed.*
- *Last time I got caught stealing a calendar I got twelve months.*
- *Having survived mustard gas and pepper spray, he's now a seasoned veteran.*

A more complex example of a pun follows:

Prince Charles returns from Africa and greets his mother, the Queen.
"What is that odd thing on your head?" she asks.
"It's a fox hat," he answers. "Don't you remember telling me that on my trip to Malawi to wear the fox hat?"

Humor

"Silly boy, when you said 'Malawi' I said, Where the fuck's that?"

Limericks are a form of poetry in five lines with a strict rhyme scheme, which is sometimes obscene, but always with humorous intent. The following example explains:

> *The limerick packs laughs anatomical*
> *into space that is quite economical.*
> *But the good ones I've seen*
> *so seldom are clean,*
> *and the clean ones so seldom are comical.*

The limerick form appeared in England in the early part of the 18th century. Edward Lear popularized it in the 19th century, and stated that the true limerick as a folk form is always obscene, and violation of taboo is part of its function. George Bernard Shaw described clean limericks as a *"fad, rarely rising above mediocrity"*. The limerick is named after an Irish city, but no one is certain why. Nevertheless, limericks have been around for more than a hundred years and remain an amusing form of humor.

Judge for yourself:

- *There once was a maid from Madras*
  who had a magnificent ass.
  Not rounded and pink,
  as you probably think,
  but gray, with long ears, and eats grass.
- *As Titian was mixing rose madder*
  his model reclined on a ladder.
  Her position to Titian
  suggested coition.
  So he climbed up the ladder and had 'er.
- *There was a young maid from Chichester*
  whose form made the saints in their niches stir.

When she knelt at her matins,
her breasts through the satins
made the Bishop of Chichester's britches stir.
- *There was a young lady named Whyte*
whose speed was much faster than light.
She set out one day
in a relative way,
and returned on the previous night.

Single-panel cartoons date back to the 19th century, are nearly all are intended for satire, caricature, or comical entertainment. In an old New Yorker cartoon a businessman stands at his desk in front of a window overlooking a city of skyscrapers. With telephone in hand, he is saying, *"No, Thursday's out. How about never—is never good for you?"* It is one of the most popular cartoons ever published and typical of the magazine's delightful humor.

Others from the New Yorker include the following:

- Eve holds an apple from the forbidden tree, while the serpent pronounces, *"Good for your heart, all the essential nutrients, controls cholesterol, and has antioxidants."*
- A chicken lies on an analyst's couch, and the doctor asks, *"Why do you think you crossed the road?"*
- Furniture is being thrown, piece by piece, from a third-story window into a truck below that has painted on its side, *"The Amazingly Inexpensive Moving Company"*

Political or editorial cartoons can usually be found on the editorial page of many newspapers, and they serve to express thoughts about current events. Most cartoons are designed to make people laugh, in an attempt to seduce rather than offend. Modern political cartooning is often built around traditional visual symbols such as Uncle Sam, the Democratic donkey and the Republican elephant. Editorial cartoons, however, are sometimes controversial enough to irritate, rather than educate.

Finally, there is the conventional one-line joke that rarely fails to bring at least a smile to all, except those over whose heads it may occasionally fly.

- *Just because nobody complains doesn't mean all parachutes are perfect.*
- *This may just be the wine talking but I really, really, really, like wine.*
- *I've decided to sell the vacuum; all it was doing was gathering dust.*
- *Say what you will about deaf people.*
- *My friend and I often laugh about how competitive we are. But I laugh more.*

As to the longer form, here are a few of those:

As a woman gets on a bus with her baby, the bus driver says, "That's the ugliest baby I've ever seen." The angry woman sits at the rear of the bus and says to the man sitting next to her, "That driver just insulted me!" The man replies, "You go right up there and tell him off! If you want, I'll hold your monkey for you."

Two men are playing golf when one notices a funeral procession passing on the adjacent road. The player who is about to tee off removes his cap, closes his eyes, and kneels down in prayer. His friend says, "That's the most touching thing I've ever seen; you are truly kind and sensitive." The other man replies, "Well, after all, we were married nearly thirty years."

A talented young chef from Beijing came to the U.S. and opened a new restaurant that succeeded beyond his dreams. He sent a message to relatives to please send an assistant, and days later a bright and lovely young woman arrived. She soon became invaluable, and the two fell in love and were married. On their wedding night the chef said, "You have brought great happiness to my life, and I wish to reciprocate. Please tell me what would bring you the greatest pleasure." She blushed and said, "I would like what I believe you call sixty-nine. "What?" the chef cried. "At a time like this you want Kung Pao Chicken with Broccoli?"

Two hunters are out in the woods when one suddenly collapses. His eyes are glazed and he doesn't seem to be breathing. The other man dials 911 on his cell phone and gasps to the operator, "My friend just collapsed; he may be dead. What can I do?" The operator says, "Calm down, I can help. First, let's make sure he's dead." There is silence, then a shot is heard. Back on the phone the hunter says, "Okay, now what?"

They say that laughter is the best medicine. It has been shown to relieve stress, decrease pain, and boost immunity. Humor, as well, lightens your burden, enhances relationships, and defuses conflicts. So for better health and endless social benefits why not put a little more humor in your life? You've nothing to lose but that frown.

Weather

Although few have the power to make things perfect, most agree we have the ability to make things better; humans have been doing that for thousands of years. The history of civilization is an endless number of small steps forward, each an improvement over what went before. After all these centuries, however, there remains one element over which we lack control and in which we have no authority, dominance, or clout whatsoever. That element is weather.

In the final World Series game played in Philadelphia, the score was tied at the end of nine exciting innings. The teams were about to begin a crucial overtime inning when it suddenly began to rain. Rain! Who needed that? Emotions were already higher than the stadium's flagpoles, and now there was a rain delay. Unplanned, unwelcome, and defying all expectations, the rains came, irritated fans groaned, and not a soul in the state of Pennsylvania, or anywhere else on earth, could do anything more about it than run for cover or open an umbrella.

Civilizations have been fascinated by weather conditions since the world began, and during most of that time people have attributed those conditions to mystical forces. Every variety of weather was thought to be the direct result of godly intervention, and every climatic element was personified as a deity to be worshiped. How else could primitive societies explain the unfathomable manifestations of nature? Some cultures offered sacrifices to honor the sun, while others danced around a campfire to bring rain. Most believed that anyone killed by a lightning strike must have angered the gods. Picture this: A poor bumpkin is quietly standing there, minding his own business. Along comes a bolt of lightning, and—just like that—he's turned into a piece of charcoal. No one will ever know if he actually offended a god, but early societies could think of no better explanation.

In Ancient Egypt, the sun took on an important religious significance. Greek mythology, as well, invented gods and goddesses that personified elements of weather. Zeus, the king of all gods, ruled the sky, including thunder, lightning, and rain. Dozens of other deities accounted for other aspects of nature. Poseidon, god of the sea, was also responsible for earthquakes. Helios was god of the sun, Selene, goddess of the moon, and the list goes on and on.

Most ancient civilizations marveled at the sun, moon and stars because of their distance, power, and regular cycles. By observing eclipses, comets, meteorites, and other phenomena, ancients related to these powerful elements as deities. African tribes adopted gods to represent natural features such as rivers, forests, and mountains, while Aztecs, Mayans, and Incans all relied heavily on the worship of celestial bodies. Some tribes actually performed human sacrifices to pacify their gods, but the notion of throwing virgins into volcanoes never happened. Sorry to say, it was a self-serving fiction created by Hollywood's creative writers.

These days we think of ancient civilizations as naïve, yet we remain in similar awe of stars, planets, comets, and especially romantic full moons. Even eclipses and the aurora borealis endure and are as breathtaking today as they were in ancient times. With so many great advances in science, the discovery of a new star these days rarely overwhelms; whereas ancients would have looked up and been perplexed by objects they could neither reach nor comprehend.

Weather is defined as what's happening in the atmosphere right now; and it includes temperature, precipitation, clouds, and wind forces. Sun provides the energy that heats the air in our atmosphere. Masses of warm and cold air then move from place to place, creating winds. It is wind currents that bring sunny, wet, or stormy conditions. So if you are unhappy with the weather, blame the sun and winds, not the TV weather person who pretends he or she has created today's climatic conditions. Forecasters may pretend to control every breeze and gust, but really, without a script they're just as befuddled as the rest of us.

The many spectacles produced by weather fascinate and often frighten people. For example, tornados are deadly twisters formed by rotating columns of wind blowing at different speeds and altitudes. You may recall that Dorothy and her dog, Toto, were caught in a spectacular tornado that transported them—as well as their entire house—to the Land of Oz.

Lightning is one of the world's wildest weather spectacles. During a thunderstorm, clouds are electrically charged, and when merged with the opposite charges of the earth's surface, white-hot lightning bolts form. Lightning is as deadly as it is impressive. Worldwide, there are about eight million lightning strikes every day. With this frequency, it's easy to understand how early cultures assumed that lightning represented a genuinely pissed off god. In fact, some still believe divine intervention caused the following examples:

During the eighteenth century lightning struck a church tower in Brescia, Italy. The current passed through the vaults where tons of gunpowder had been stored for safekeeping. The aftermath destroyed a sixth of the city and killed 3,000 residents.

In 1963, lightning hit a Pan American Boeing 707 en route from Puerto Rico to Philadelphia. The bolt struck the left wing, igniting the fuel vapor mixture stored in a reserve fuel tank. The airplane exploded in midair, killing every passenger aboard.

Chaos hit New York City in 1977 when lightning struck the Consolidated Edison electrical transmission line in Westchester County. The strike short-circuited major transmission lines and power was out for 25 hours. People were trapped in subways and elevators, and looting, rioting, and arson erupted throughout the city.

Now for the good news: 70 percent of people who get hit by lightning survive. Victims often claim to suffer physical changes, such as memory loss, depression, blurred vision, and occasional impotence. *"So when you hear it thunder,"* as the Johnny Burke lyrics go, *"don't run under a tree..."* A better strategy is to go back in the house and dive under your bed.

Like many others, I have personally witnessed a number of

frightening, weather-related phenomena. I grew up in the Midwest, where electrical storms were common, and hearing thunder at an early age was a terrifying experience. It sounded like a sonic boom coming through the front door. This was shortly followed by a blinding klieg light that illuminated the entire neighborhood. It is little wonder ancients believed the gods were angry; as a little kid, I thought the world was coming to an end.

My next experience was as a young seaman when our ship ran into the tail end of a hurricane off the Brazilian coast. The waters became violent, the shrieking wind was deafening, and our ship felt perilously out of control. I felt little danger, but rather excitement, as I went on deck to view the spectacle first hand. After opening a door on the leeward side I was flattened by a gust that threw me down like a three-hundred-pound linebacker had just tackled me. I was immediately soaked by the wind-swept spray and for several minutes was unable to move. I was suddenly lifted by a deck hand who said, "What the fuck's the matter with you; are you fuckin' crazy? Get your fuckin' ass below and stay there until this fuckin' weather passes." And that's how shipmates—even today—communicate heartfelt concern for each other during perilous incidents.

The Bel-Air Fire was a disaster that began as a brush fire in November 1961, and was at the time the worst fire in the history of Los Angeles. The fire was fueled by a strong Santa Ana wind condition, as well as tinder-dry foliage. Nearly 500 homes were destroyed, 16,000 acres burned, and thousands of people were forced to evacuate their homes. Given the exclusive neighborhood's location in Los Angeles, there were numerous celebrities whose homes were burned to the ground.

The first house I designed and built was located in a canyon adjacent to Bel-Air.

When I rushed home from the office I saw flames at the top of the street moving from Bel-Air towards my house. There was barely time to load the car with family and a few possessions before leaving. We returned the following day to discover that the fire had reversed course only three houses uphill from ours. We suffered no loss, but gained great respect for the incredible power of nature.

Weather

Finally, the 6.7-magnitude Northridge Earthquake struck close to our home in January 1994. It still stands as the second costliest disaster in U.S. history, second only to Hurricane Katrina. The quake killed 57 people, injured thousands more, damaged 112,000 structures, and left more than $20 billion in property losses. More than 20,000 people were displaced from their homes, and probably double that number began to wish they lived anywhere else on earth.

The jolt hit Los Angeles' San Fernando Valley at 4:30 a.m. We were rudely awakened that morning when our bed rose in the air and crashed back down to the floor. It seemed the violent shaking would last forever, but it quickly stopped. As we surveyed the damage by flashlight we saw cracked plaster walls everywhere, books, lamps, TVs, and other objects littered the floors, and the kitchen looked like a war zone, with broken glasses, dishes, and our entire wine supply running wild in an alcoholic stream. Actually, we were lucky; our brick chimney was the only one on the block left standing, but cracks appeared throughout the property.

And now a few words about global warming: The overwhelming weight of scientific evidence collected to date shows that climate change is one of the greatest threats to humans today. Examples of current catastrophic effects include loss of polar ice cap, rising sea levels, increasing global temperatures, and escalating frequency and intensity of natural disasters.

Since the increased use of fossil fuels has been identified as the main cause of global warming it is not surprising that those connected to the fossil fuel industry are the most vocal opponents of the global warming notion. "It's a hoax", they claim, inferring that scientists are part of an elaborate scheme to intentionally mislead the public using 'fictitious' or modified climate data. Believe what you will, but if 97 percent of the world's research scientists agree that global warming is a real threat, I believe you'd be foolish to stick your head in the sand.

Weather remains a crucial part of our lives, as it always has. Destructive weather can mean losses of property and life, while fine weather conditions grow the crops on which we depend. We know more about meteorology now than we did a thousand years ago, but there is much about nature that is as mysterious and awe-inspiring today as it has ever been.

Before meteorologists, people made forecasts based on observation of the sky and nature. For example:

- *The higher the clouds, the finer the weather.*
- *Clear moon—frost soon.*
- *Spiders spinning large webs are signs of a harsh winter.*
- *Red sky at morning, sailors take warning.*
- *Ring around the moon—rain real soon.*

Weather forecasts are important as they determine when crops are planted, watered, and harvested. Forecasts also help us plan what to wear, when to travel, and when to turn off your sprinkler system. They are especially important for farmers, builders, sailors, and anyone else working outdoors. Forecasts are based on the information meteorologists receive about air temperature, wind speeds, clouds, and rainfall from over 50,000 weather stations worldwide on land, ships, and buoys at sea. This data is fed into huge computers that produce charts and forecasts. These are used—with satellite images—to predict the weather.

Other natural predictors, often disregarded as unreliable, are those who respond to changes in humidity and barometric pressure. They say, "I feel it in my bones". Every so often it will actually rain, but at other times, it's just the arthritis talking.

An old native of Idaho once declared he had developed an absolutely foolproof method for determining the weather. Referring to a neat pile of rocks near his front porch, he said, "When the rocks are dry, the weather is fair. When the rocks are wet, it's raining. When the rocks are white, it's snowing. And when the rocks disappear, it's snowing heavily."

Others say, "Why not tune in the 24-hour Weather Channel? Or easier yet, just look out the window."

Sports

Prehistoric hunters threw spears at wild animals, but not for sport; their hope was to provide a tasty dinner for their cave-mates. If the spear missed its mark, however, the hunter was obliged to run like crazy to avoid becoming the *animal's* dinner. Throwing spears and running fast in those days were basic survival tactics. Today, we no longer hunt to eat; yet the sport of javelin throwing requires skills comparable to prehistoric hunters. And running swiftly, once motivated by mortal fear, is prompted these days by the competitive desire to win a medal.

Sports began as a means to develop skills required for hunting and waging war. Ancient cave paintings in France depict people sprinting and wrestling, while artistic images in Libya indicate that swimming and archery were practiced thousands of years ago. Even activities, like rowing and weightlifting, are portrayed in centuries old Egyptian hieroglyphics.

Ancient Greeks formalized sports when they originated the first Olympic games nearly three thousand years ago. The games were held every four years and consisted initially of a single sprinting event. Olympic sports gradually expanded to include other events, and today the two-week-long spectacle, watched by billions of people worldwide, features more than two dozen sports ranging from water polo and canoeing to gymnastics and tennis.

We are all drawn to sports early in life, and children at the age of five or six are already wearing team logos, while rooting for their favorite players. When did this all begin? Children have always played competitive games, but the mandatory-schooling movement in the 19th

119

century created a schedule that included free periods of recess, where boys and girls could run around the schoolyard, as well as compete in after-school games.

Sports are considered important in teaching essential values. First, playing sports is fun and offers a way to make friends with teammates, while developing leadership skills. Youngsters learn that sometimes you win and sometimes you lose, and there is a preferred way to deal with success as well as disappointment. Finally, studies show that those involved in sports are more likely to have high self-esteem, academic success, and better overall health; and they are less likely to be overweight or do drugs. Considering the benefits, one wonders why youngsters don't turn off the TV more often and go outside to shoot a few baskets.

On the other hand, there are those who inevitably go overboard. They are the ones who enroll their children in Little League Baseball, Pee Wee hockey, or Pop Warner football. These are nationally organized youth sports programs designed to encourage a child's participation in competitions on a national scale. But here's the problem: Some eager parents show up at a game, scream directions to their poor kid, ignore the coach, embarrass the child, and treat a win or loss as if it were life or death. These are little kids, after all, doing their best; and the parent is acting like a total fool. If you are one of these parents, please, grow up and stop acting like an idiot!

Youngsters who survive early sports experiences often continue with one sport or another for much of their lives. Some star on high school teams, possibly get a scholarship to play on a college team, and a rare few become successful, professional athletes. Others, like me, go out for high school football, try to tackle a furious running back during a practice game, and get a mild concussion, putting a sad end to a sports career that never stood a chance. Worse yet was the parental lecture that followed.

"What were you thinking?" asked my distraught mother. "We didn't raise you to play football. If you want to play something, take up the violin." Later in life I discovered tennis, where the risk of concussion is slight, helmets are not required, and the pleasure of the game can continue until you're ready for assisted living, or perhaps have a coronary arguing a bad line call.

Since the advent of cable television, there has been an explosive interest in sports. Today there are more than forty cable channels devoted exclusively to sports, ranging from football and tennis to cricket and ice hockey, plus what I call the *going-around-sports*–auto racing, horse racing, and cycling. The millions of advertising dollars generated by sports have lifted the salaries of sports participants to unbelievable levels. For example, the sum of salary, bonus, and endorsements for Cristiano Ronaldo, the Portuguese soccer player, is 88 million dollars a year, LeBron James earns 77 million playing basketball, and Phil Mickelson plays several rounds of golf for a cool 53 million. I know, I know, their professional years are limited, but in a single year they earn enough to retire to an island in the Caribbean for the rest of their lives.

In addition to receiving advertising income, sport teams now charge incredible prices to attend sporting events. The cheapest resale ticket at the 2016 World Series games in Chicago was $2200. If you took a friend and both had a couple of hotdogs and beers, and threw in a logo cap or two, you're looking to drop close to $5000! That may sound a bit steep, but it was peanuts compared to a seat in the second row behind the Cub's dugout; each of those seats went for $24,000! Even in Philadelphia, where the final game was played, the worst seat went for $1400.

By comparison, your outrageous cable bill–perhaps a couple of hundred dollars a month– is a screaming bargain. Just think, on a recent Saturday there were thirty-six individual college football games being broadcast, plus twenty worldwide soccer games. And that doesn't count dozens more action programs, including golf, cliff diving, boxing, and the world series of poker. All this happened on just one day! When does a sports enthusiast find time over the weekend to mow the lawn, or even take out the trash?

Despite the prevalence of sports in our life, there are some who remain oblivious to the action surrounding them. They may watch a Super Bowl once a year, or perhaps the opening ceremonies of the Olympics, but they often prefer to see a play, go to a concert, or stay home, turn off the TV, and read a book. Before criticizing any of those types, we should remember that the Declaration of Independence affirms our inalienable right to the pursuit of happiness. So, while many enjoy sports, others have every inalienable right to happiness by ignoring the fervor, the mayhem, and the circus atmosphere.

Sportsmanship strives for fair play, ethical behavior, and grace in victory and defeat. The modern Olympic creed proposes that, *"The most important thing is not winning, but in taking part."* The sports journalist, Grantland Rice said, *"It's not that you won or lost but how you played the game."* Vince Lombardi, coach of the Green Bay Packers believed, *"Winning isn't everything, it's the only thing."* And Red Symons, the Australian writer and composer alleged, *"Winning is not everything, but losing is nothing."*

So there you have it—a variety of attitudes on the relative importance of winning. Of course, every athlete wants to win, but in any contest involving two teams only one generally wins, and among the losers, some are inevitably more gracious than others.

Cheating in sports sometimes happen. Though rules are in place to ensure fair play, and officials are invariably impartial, rules are occasionally broken to gain an advantage. There have been cases where a game has been "fixed", boxers may "take a dive", and the outcome has been predetermined—all of this because of gambling money. Doping and drugs are another way to distort a contest's outcome. Athletes in a variety of sports have been caught taking performance-enhancing drugs, and when caught have suffered punishment, as well as embarrassment.

Just as loving spouses may at times cheat, athletes sometimes fail to live up to the expectations of their teams. We are all less than perfect, but because the will to win is so powerful some ignore the spirit of what it means to act honorably. A famous coach once said, "It was not cheating, it was creative winning", which in itself, is a pretty creative interpretation. In non-professional sports as well, we often find the occasional tennis player, for example, that gives dreadful line calls. A ball falling a foot within the line is called "out", and all one can do is suggest the player see an ophthalmologist before he or she walks into a tree.

Sports

Violence in sports involves crossing the line between fair competition and intentional aggression. Athletes, coaches, and fans, sometimes unleash violent behavior on people or property in misguided displays of loyalty, anger, or celebration. The author George Orwell once observed, *"Serious sport has nothing to do with fair play. It is bound up with hatred, jealousy, boastfulness, disregard of all rules and sadistic pleasure in witnessing violence; in other words it is war minus the shooting."*

Contact sports, such as football, ice hockey, and boxing involve certain levels of physical violence, but restrictions and penalties are applied for excessive and dangerous use of force. Physically aggressive acts, like legal blocks in football and body checks in ice hockey, can be brutally violent actions, yet both are within the rules of the games and not intended to injure. Not particularly so with mixed marshal arts, which is a full contact sport that combines boxing, wrestling, kick boxing, jiu-jitsu, and almost any other grappling and striking skill. Detractors have called these bouts "human cockfights" and proposed a ban, but the popularity of these fights has only risen with each bloody encounter.

Violence appears to be socially acceptable–a part of the game, so to speak–and it seems to define who we have become as a nation forever at war. Those who take part in contact sports realize there are risks of physical injury, similar to other risky sports such as skiing, snowboarding, and motorcycle racing. All sports may involve aggressive tactics, but actual violence is often ignored, and not always considered unsportsmanlike.

Speaking of violence, there is nothing today anything like sporting entertainment in ancient Rome. Nothing even close. Gladiators fought to the death before an audience. The objective was not a quick kill but rather to trap the opponent and extend the fight long enough to please the crowd. The combatants, who knew this might be their last day, circled one another jabbing swords and swinging maces.

Suddenly, one gladiator might trap the other with a net and be poised to kill him with a deadly trident. The victor waited for a sign from the crowd. If the losing gladiator put up a good fight, the crowd might give thumbs up, choose to spare his life, and the vanquished gladiator would live to fight another day. But if the crowd was dissatisfied with the loser—as was usually the case—dissatisfaction meant slaughter.

Another bit of gory entertainment was the not-so-sporting diversion of watching people suffer an agonizing death when thrown into an amphitheater with wild animals. Early Christians were often the victims of this terrible fate, and one wonders how anyone in the audience could continue snacking on their figs and olives while this kind of bloody mayhem was going on.

On a more optimistic note, the best moments in sports are those that are unexpected, and that's what makes underdog stories so magical. Few events capture one's imagination like a gutsy athlete or team pulling off a massive upset over what looks like an unbeatable opponent. It's a story that resonates for decades and inspires others to attempt similar astonishing feats.

The 1980 United States Olympic Hockey Team's victory over the Soviet Union was selected by Sports Illustrated as one of the greatest sporting events of all-time and the finest sports moment of the 20th century. It was called the "Miracle on Ice".

Throughout the history of the Winter Games, Americans had won a single gold medal. Entering the 1980 Olympics, the hockey team was seeded seventh in the 12-nation pool, a decided underdog. The team's coach was Herb Brooks, the University of Minnesota's hockey coach. Among the twenty young players he selected, twelve were native Minnesotans, and he had previously coached nine of those players.

The U.S. tied Sweden in the opening game. They then upset the Czechoslovakian team, and proceeded to beat Norway and Rumania. Only West Germany stood in their way to compete in the medal round, and on late goals, the U.S. won that game, giving them a date with the mighty Soviets. Russia, the defending champion, had won the Olympic gold medal five of the last six times, and up to that point, had outscored their opponents 51-11 through the first five games. No one believed the Americans had even the slightest chance.

The game had unimaginable hype, including political and social implications. The U.S. scored first, and three minutes later the Soviets answered. They outshot the U.S., but by the final period the game was tied 3-3. Midway through the period, team captain Mike Eruzione fired "the shot heard round the world." The U.S. led 4-3.

The final ten minutes of the game was as stressful as watching a snail cross a highway, but the Americans held on. As the crowd counted down the final seconds, the announcer, Al Michaels, shouted, *"Do you believe in miracles?"* And with that extraordinary game the Americans made it into the gold medal final, beating Finland and concluding one of the most unlikely events in sports history.

And that is why dedicated fans watch televised sports; to be there when miracles happen.

Lies & Liars

Everybody lies. Yes, everybody! You, me, the cop on the beat, the guy in the pulpit, and even your trusted auto mechanic who claims you're facing certain death if you don't replace your fuel pump immediately. Some people admit they exaggerate or embellish or lay it on pretty thick, and "What's so wrong with that," they ask? Well, here's what's wrong with that: Call it what you will—it's lying.

People have always lied. More than three thousand years ago Moses brought down from Mount Sinai the Ten Commandments from God. We can only guess how unruly life must have been to prescribe prohibitions against murder, thievery, adultery, coveting anything belonging to your neighbor, and not least of all—lying.

The ninth commandment tells us that speaking with the intention to deceive others is what constitutes a lie. By a glance of the eye, a motion of the hand, or a facial expression, a lie may be told as effectively as by words. An intentional overstatement or insinuation calculated to convey an erroneous impression, as well as the omission of facts to mislead, is also lying. Any manipulation of a fact to produce a particular result is a violation of the ninth commandment.

Regardless of what you may believe, the ninth commandment leaves no room for doubt; exaggeration, overstatement, and misrepresentation—they are all lies. How can we possibly get through the day without even the most innocent of falsehoods? For example, when asked how we are, we say, "Fine," but we often ignore the argument we had with our spouse that morning, including the slammed door, which made us feel

127

anything but fine. And what about that annoying touch of constipation? Do you call that "fine"? Forget it; that's nobody else's business.

Is it possible that one could tell the absolute truth at all times? Unlikely, I think, because you'd have to be truly eccentric to pull that off. In the 1944 play "Harvey" by Mary Chase, the hero, Elwood P. Dowd, always told the truth and was nearly committed to an asylum by his embarrassed sister. Of course, his odd best friend, Harvey, was a six-foot-tall white rabbit that nobody else could see, and that didn't help. But never uttering a word that wasn't the absolute truth was considered pathologically abnormal.

Some lies, of course, are worse than others. If you tell someone asking for a donation to The Children's Aid Society that you gave at the office, when in fact you didn't, it's not as serious as claiming a Mid-east country has weapons of mass destruction. Nevertheless, even a white lie is a lie, and that realization should certainly prompt a twinge of remorse.

Most children learn to lie by the age of four or five. That's about the time they discover how extensively you've lied to them. Santa Claus coming down the chimney? Money under the pillow left by the Tooth Fairy? Rabbits delivering Easter treats? You're lucky they're even speaking to you. Like the rest of us, children lie to conceal or mislead. For example, they might claim they washed their hands or deny they ate the cookie, when all evidence points to the contrary. In time they become more skillful, and years later may tell the Highway Patrolman they had only a small apéritif before dinner, which caused them to weave a slalom-like course down the highway.

Some lies have become so popular they have become punch lines to jokes or even jokes in themselves. Consider the following:

- From your trusted dentist: *"This won't hurt a bit."*
- From the insolvent borrower: *"The check is in the mail."*
- From a dutiful husband to his obese wife: *"The miniskirt looks great on you."*
- From the maître d': *"Your table will be ready any minute."*
- From the husband covered with lipstick: *"I swear she's only a friend."*

- From the seducer: *"Of course I'll respect you in the morning."*
- From almost any student: *"The dog ate my homework."*

Self-serving lies are the most common form of lying. They are motivated by a desire to avoid unpleasant situations or protect another person's feelings. Let's say your new girlfriend has cooked her first dinner for you, but the lamb chop tastes like cardboard and the mashed potatoes have more lumps than Quasimodo. What do you say? "Sorry, honey, it's pretty obvious you're a lousy cook." Perhaps not–she may realize herself the food is awful. Better to say, "I'm really impressed by what you've done," which is simply a white lie of omission. Why say more and embarrass her? Unless, of course, her cooking is a deal-breaker, and it's the perfect time to say *adios*.

Another potentially awkward situation is when going backstage to greet an actor friend who has just given the worst performance of his life in one of the most dreadful plays ever written. What can you possibly say? Another actor friend suggests this: Smile broadly, put your arm around his shoulder, and say with great sincerity, "You son-of-a-gun!"

Lying is a form of cheating, and those that doctor their résumés with past honors and letters of commendation are clearly lying to appear more appealing and deserving of a particular position. Or perhaps they lie about their age or ignore the arrest for peddling drugs some years ago. So what's wrong with juicing up the résumé or avoiding shameful details, you might ask? Just this; you're misrepresenting, deceiving, and no two ways about it–lying. It's the same as claiming you graduated from Harvard or Yale, rather than the Gerhard Schnitzel Technical School of Automotive Repair.

Not all deception is a lie. Camouflage, for example, is meant to deceive the enemy, and that's a good thing. So is plastic surgery, in which the deception is used for personal improvement, just as are false eyelashes or a little padding here or there. Deception of this sort is considered socially acceptable and often appropriate.

There should actually be an entire encyclopedia devoted to the Advertising Industry, Car Salespeople, and Politicians. These are areas where compulsive liars and pathological lying flourish. Let's begin with the most innocent of lies: The neighborhood coffee shop with the exterior sign that declares, *"Voted Best Breakfast in Town"*. To be fair, the waffles are okay, and the eggs are fresh, but "Best in Town"? So I asked the waitress, "Who exactly voted for your breakfast?" And she answered, "We've been trying to figure that one out. I have a hunch the owner and his six kids each voted a few times."

National advertisers, on the other hand, wantonly exaggerate and mislead on an almost daily basis. For example, *Airborn*, an herbal supplement, claimed to ward off bacteria and germs that cause common colds. Not so, as it turned out, and the company settled for $23 million in a class action lawsuit.

Splenda, a sugar substitute, was advertised as "made from actual sugar", whereas it was proved to be a highly processed chemical compound made in a factory. The final settlement was confidential.

Activa yogurt claimed nutritional benefits beyond all other yogurts, but was found to be virtually identical to other yogurts. During the ensuing class action settlement the company paid out $45 million.

Hundai overstated the horsepower of some vehicles and ended up paying about $75 million to settle complaints.

Finally, *Extenze* claimed it was *"scientifically proven to increase certain male body parts."* The company settled for $6 million paid to sadly disappointed and insufficiently endowed men throughout the country.

Here's one that's really hard to beat: A recent Christmas gift catalog advertised a Homemade Gin Kit with the accompanying description, *"Craft your own blend of gin with this all-in-one kit. Just add vodka."* I'm sure nothing like this has been seen since Jesus turned water into wine.

It is difficult to understand why car salespeople find it necessary to lie. Other salespeople may exaggerate or mislead as well, but car salespeople have become genius manipulators in an almost Machiavellian fashion.

My own experience is personal proof that car people have little regard for the truth. I noticed that all the cars I viewed had a small strip of metal, called a spoiler, on the trunk lid. Most racecars have spoilers, but I wasn't buying a racecar, and in my opinion the spoiler was aptly named; it actually spoiled the car's design.

"Is the spoiler essential," I asked?

"Yes," answered the salesman, "It's a stock item, and all cars come that way." Then I noticed the inventory of details on the side window, and the spoiler was listed for an extra $115.

"Why would you list the spoiler as an extra if it's a stock item," I asked?

Ignoring the question, the salesperson said, "We can have it removed, if you like."

Then I asked why I had to purchase the highly sophisticated sound system, which was listed for an additional couple of hundred dollars. Couldn't I just get a simple radio?

The salesperson said, "If you don't get the sound system that comes with the car you won't have a radio."

"What kind of car these days comes *without* a radio," I asked? The salesperson said, "Excuse me for a minute," and then he walked away. I asked to see the manager and we discussed the radio issue. "He may not have understood you," said the manager.

When the salesperson returned I said, "Thanks for your help, but I'm not buying a car from you. Would you like to know why?" He nodded. "It's because you seem to have trouble telling the truth. I can't trust anything you say, so I'm going to another dealer." He barely registered surprise or disappointment, as if this happened several times a day.

Politicians? They all lie; every last one of them. That's just the way they are. Yes, that applies to George Washington and Abraham Lincoln, as well. Do you recall the story of the cherry tree? The young Washington allegedly said, *"I cannot tell a lie, father, I cut down your cherry tree."* It's a wonderful and inspirational story about the innate honesty of our first president, but sorry to say, it never happened; it was totally fabricated.

How about Honest Abe? He believed, and famously said, *"All men are created equal."* But in order to get elected he also said, *"I am not in favor of bringing about in any way the social and political equality of the white and black races—nor have I been in favor of making voters or jurors of negroes, nor to intermarry with white people. In addition, there are differences between the white and black races which I believe will forever*

forbid the two races living together on terms of social and political equality."
So much for the honest face on the five-dollar bill—the historic hero
credited with freeing the slaves.

So why do politicians lie? According to those who do, it's not really
a lie they are telling; it's a deception, a bit of fact bending, misdirection,
half-truth perhaps, and worst of all, an alternative truth, but it's never
a lie. Politicians may misspeak, exaggerate, or their words may be
distorted, taken out of context, or maliciously misconstrued. But do
they lie? Never!

As to the political flip-flop, the sudden change of opinion on a
political matter, politicians may get away with it by convincing voters
that a genuine change of heart has taken place—an epiphany, so to speak.
However, flip-flopping is a dangerous exploit that sometimes backfires—
similar to a sky diving effort gone wrong.

Most politicians are narcissists who often display arrogance, self-
importance, and a healthy sense of entitlement. They generally believe
they are right even when they know in their hearts they are wrong.
However, devoted followers tend to trust everything a politician says,
because many people don't want to hear the truth. Voters want to hear
what they have always believed to be true, and when politicians feed
that belief by lying to them, voters are satisfied. If candidate "A" tells the
truth and candidate "B" tells the public what it wants to hear, candidate
"B" will win in a landslide. Essentially, dishonesty is the best policy for
getting elected.

If a lie is told repeatedly people assume it's true. No less a prevaricator
than Adolph Hitler once stated, *"If you make it big, make it simple, and
keep saying it—eventually they will believe it."* Thus, it has often been said
that pretty words are not always true, nor are true words always pretty.

Fashion

Let's assume it's a typical workday. You're up early browsing through the closet trying to decide what to wear to work. Suddenly it hits you; nothing hanging there is very appealing. You don't even recognize half the clothes. Who bought these rags, and what are they doing in your closet? You may think this is strictly a female problem, but men, as well as women, suffer over choosing something flattering to wear—the sort of outfit that puts your best foot forward, rather than an outfit that accentuates those unsightly bulges.

Some people have it easy; those in the armed forces, for example, have little choice; it's khaki, camouflage, or a classic sailor suit. And doctors aren't especially concerned, since their white coats cover up God only knows what? Most laborers, like auto mechanics, gardeners, and plumbers, wear work clothes that serve as unofficial uniforms. And those working at home don't really care what they wear, because no one—except perhaps the mailperson—will ever see them. So they may schlump around in a bathrobe and sloppy slippers, or perhaps an athletic outfit more suitable for a yoga class.

Then, of course, there are a few who are totally oblivious to what they wear. If it passes the maximum gravy spot limit and olfactory test it's perfectly acceptable. So what if the colors and patterns clash like thunder and lightning? Who cares? These folks are considered eccentrics, marching through life to their own sightless drumbeat. Most of us who work with others, on the other hand, want to make a good impression by appearing as fashionably dressed as possible. This may take a few more minutes each day, but the result can make your image, and consequently your life, more appealing.

Where did this all come from, and why do we invest so much energy and suffer such angst about the way we dress? Believe it or not, it all started with Adam and Eve. There they were, two free spirits running around Eden and having the time of their lives. Then one day the serpent suggested that Eve take a bite of the apple hanging from the forbidden Tree of Knowledge. This was the tree, God warned, whose fruit was prohibited, because it would open their eyes to good and evil.

Eve yielded to the crafty serpent's urging, took a bite of the fruit, shared the apple with Adam, and both acquired the wisdom that god had forbidden. With open eyes, they suddenly realized their nakedness, and they became aware of physical lust.

Good for them, you might think, but no—they also became aware of their guilt. Realizing it was now inappropriate to remain unclothed, they quickly covered up with fashion-forward fig-leaf bikinis, and the free and easy days became but a fond memory. Worse yet, they had to find a new place to live, as God, their landlord, banished them from Eden. This entire episode, known as "Original Sin", refers to the violation of disobeying God's command. So, if it were not for the serpent, the apple, and all that followed, chances are we'd all be running around naked, and deciding what to wear would be the least of our worries.

Okay, that's really not the whole story. Prehistoric people, who some believe predate Adam and Eve, began covering up perhaps 100,000 years ago as protection from the elements. That probably coincided with the migration of tribes north from their origins in Africa. Of course, clothing does more these days than protect us from weather. It identifies sex, occupation, individual preferences, and in many societies it reflects the standards of modesty, religion, and social status. Consider, for example the dictate in many Islamic nations of women totally covering every part of the body, except the eyes. The exception of the eyes is probably to protect women from walking into open manholes. The total covering is both religious and social in nature and intended to keep the sexual appetites of passing men at bay when traveling outside the home. This might even save a woman's life, since she is usually assumed to bear the responsibility of unlawful sexual encounters and thus, subject to stoning. Yes, this kind of nonsense still persists—even in the 21ˢᵗ century!

Clothing, for most of us, functions as an expression of personal taste or style. But what you wear also reveals who you are or who you want to be. It informs others of your ambitions, emotions, and social status. We rely on clothing as an economic and social indicator because our society has no other measure of rank or status. There are few aristocracies these days, where royals dressed elegantly and peasants dressed, well, like peasants. Any American today can dress like a prince or princess or even a lowly serf, regardless of actual wealth, social position, or common sense.

There is definitely a psychology of dress that determines our clothing choices. Some dress shabbily because that's the way they feel about themselves; others dress provocatively, wishing to project a decidedly erotic image. Consciously or otherwise we all dress the way we wish to be considered. Actors long ago discovered that putting on a costume enabled the expression of a character. The same is true of us all in everyday life. In a way, every day could very well be Halloween; one day you're royalty, another day a woman of the night, or perhaps a colorful clown in a traveling circus.

Wardrobe preferences are developed over the years to express who we are. A few wardrobe habits, however, have led to unintended consequences. Some are listed below, including suggestions for those who may wish to reconsider:

- Keeping every piece of clothing you've ever owned may suggest you're clinging to the past. You might consider giving away a few things to your favorite charity.
- Dressing in clothing too large for your body may be an attempt to hide your actual figure. Perhaps losing some weight and buying better fitting outfits is the answer.
- Covering yourself in design logos suggests the need to express wealth, in order to impress others. Try wearing something elegant and lose the logos.

- Dressing inappropriately sexy is often an attempt to gain attention. You might consider if that's really the image you wish to project.
- Dressing too young for your age fools no one. Your age is what it is, and wearing age-appropriate classic outfits will produce a far more appealing image.

Fashion and style are two different matters. Fashion relates to the external, what's happening on the runways in New York, Paris, or Milan. Fashion dictates whether hemlines are high or low, whether lapels are wide or narrow, and the proper widths of ties and bell-bottoms. Style, on the other hand, relates to the internal–your perception of who you are. The designer, Rachel Zoe, said that, *"Style is a way to say who you are without having to speak."* While the emphasis of fashion is on items deemed fashionable, the emphasis of style is on you, the person. As Coco Chanel maintained, *"Fashion fades, but only style remains the same."*

There is no one style that will automatically make you appear more beautiful, more charming, or more successful. Each person eventually finds the "look" that expresses what he or she wishes to project. Or not. Some go through life searching and ultimately discarding one image after another, never certain, but always dissatisfied with their appearance. And sadly, there are some who have no idea what I'm talking about, or could they care less. They are satisfied with their appearance, and they might very well think you and your fashion police can take a long walk off a short pier.

The fashion designer, Betsey Johnson, suggests that women should dress to please themselves first, and then consider those with whom they must deal on a regular basis. In other words, you must be comfortable in your wardrobe choices and not pander to fashion experts or be swayed by the latest photos in gossip magazines. *"Otherwise, if girls dressed only for boys, they'd just walk around naked all the time."*

Women often seem unaware of the effect when wearing very short skirts or plunging necklines; while men are equally ignorant of the effect of hip-hugging, baggy jeans, shirts open to the waist, and tone-deaf color combinations. It may be a temporary social rebellion, but negative images remains long after the person decides to rejoin society. Other statements these days are made by those who wear images or messages on their T-shirts. Few seem to resist becoming a walking billboard, even when the message is annoying or in bad taste. Some recent examples from actual T-shirts explain more convincingly:

- I LOOK BETTER NAKED
- 6 OUT OF 7 DWARFS ARE NOT HAPPY
- MY HUSBAND'S WIFE IS AWESOME
- I MAY BE WRONG, BUT I DOUBT IT
- YES, THEY'RE REAL
- WHO CARES WHAT YOU THINK?

It's my personal view that there's entirely too much communication going on. When walking down the street and being assailed by endless personal messages, there is an overwhelming urge to shout, "Enough already; now kindly, shut up!" And while we're at it, another irritation is baseball hats worn backwards. Do these people realize how foolish they look? The purpose of the brim is to keep sun out of your eyes, not off the back of your neck. If this is just a juvenile protest, it's time to grow up! Yes, professional tennis players—you, too.

Some years ago, fashion was considerably more formal. Watch a few old movies and you'll discover that both men and women rarely left home without wearing a hat. Men also wore ties almost everywhere, except to bed, of course. The actor, Clark Gable, who starred in the 1934 movie "It Happened One Night", and incidentally earned an Academy Award for his part, made a singular fashion statement. After Gable removed his shirt to reveal a bare chest in a famous scene with Claudette Colbert, American men abandoned undershirts in droves, so much so that undershirt sales declined by seventy-five percent. Undergarment manufacturers were devastated, and the industry didn't recover until World War II uniforms got men back into the undershirt habit. Such is the power of fashion when endorsed by famous people.

Many still find fashion inspiration from popular movies, TV

shows, red-carpet appearances, or even a day at the beach. Inspiration is everywhere, and designers are constantly under pressure to produce new clothing lines for every season of the year. If you try to keep up with the latest look you will end up shopping continuously and eventually flirt with bankruptcy.

Finally, a few words about the famous, French fashion icon, Coco Chanel. Chanel was born in France in 1883 and raised in an orphanage by nuns who taught her to sew, a skill that would lead to her life's work. As a young woman, Chanel had a brief career as a singer. During that period she changed her name from Gabrielle to Coco, a shortened version of "cocotte", the French word for "kept woman".

Chanel opened her first shop, selling hats, in 1910. Her first clothing success came from a dress she fashioned out of an old jersey. The dress became hugely popular, and the talented designer was on her way. Ten years later she launched the perfume, Chanel No. 5, which became—and remains today—incredibly popular. Chanel said, *"Perfume is the unseen, unforgettable, ultimate accessory of fashion that heralds your arrival and prolongs your departure"*.

The legendary Chanel suit was introduced in 1925; the revolutionary design featured a collarless jacket and well-fitted skirt. Another revolutionary design was the little black dress. Chanel took a color associated with mourning and showed how chic it could be for eveningwear. These two designs remain today as popular as ever. She was quoted as saying about her designs, *"Simplicity is the keynote of true elegance."*

Coco Chanel died in 1971 at her long-time Paris apartment at the Hotel Ritz. Though she was pursued and loved by many prominent men, she never married. Hundreds gathered at the Church of the Madeleine to bid farewell to the fashion icon, many wearing their Chanel suits in tribute. She is remembered for her enormous influence on the world of fashion, her timeless designs, and not least of all by her many pronouncements, one of the most perceptive of which was, *"The best things in life are free, but the second best are incredibly expensive."*

Anger

"Network" was a 1976 film written by Paddy Chayefsky and directed by Sidney Lumet. The story concerns a fictional television network and its struggle with poor ratings. Howard Beale, longtime anchor of the network's Evening News, played by the actor Peter Finch, hears he will be fired in two weeks because of declining ratings. The following night, Beale announces on live television that he will commit suicide on next Tuesday's broadcast. The following day he promises to apologize for his dramatic outburst, but once on the air, he launches into a powerful tirade that causes ratings to spike and the unlikely Beale to become a populist hero and network savior. The speech remains today a classic example of pure, unadulterated anger.

Beale's emotional complaint is that living conditions have become intolerable and there is no hope for improvement. People are out of work or frightened of losing their jobs; the air is unfit to breathe, our food unfit to eat, and worse yet, nobody knows what to do about it. Violence is on the rise, punks are running wild in the streets, and conditions have become so dangerous people don't go out anymore. They sit in their houses, their world becomes smaller, and all they want is to be left alone while trying to ignore the craziness going on around them.

Beale cannot leave them alone, however; he wants them to get mad. First, you've got to get mad. You've gotta say, *"I'm a human being, goddammit! My life has value!"*

Beale becomes increasingly agitated and finally raises his voice to a crescendo level. In a desperate appeal he urges his audience to get up out of their chairs. *"Go to the window and open it,"* he says. *"Stick your*

*head out and yell, I'M AS MAD AS HELL, AND I'M NOT GOING
TO TAKE THIS ANYMORE!!"*

If you think that sounds dramatic, you should watch the movie
and see for yourself the power of Peter Finch's performance. It was so
incredibly compelling it led to a Best Actor Academy Award.

At one time or another I think we've all felt like the Howard Beale
character. Many of the irritations he ranted about decades ago remain
with us today, and the level of frustration and pure anger may be even
greater. A recent Esquire/NBC survey found that half of all Americans
are angrier today than they were just a year ago, and it's not getting
better. So what's everybody so angry about? As it turns out, just about
everything. Many think the American Dream is dead, that our country's
role in the world is not what it used to be, and most lives are not working
out the way we imagined they would. And that's why a majority of
people today view life as disappointing and depressing.

When we think things should get better, it's frustrating when they
do not. More than 80% of Americans say they're worried about the
economy, even though our economy is growing and unemployment is
low. Family income today, adjusted for inflation, is about the same as
it was twenty years ago, while inequality is worse. Yes, the rich have
gotten richer and corporations are earning record profits, but inequality
today is as bad as it was in the 1920s. The top 10% of income earners in
America take home a record 50% of all income. Meanwhile, the number
of destitute and homeless people across the country is growing larger
every day. It's that sort of inequality that makes people angry.

People are also angry about random shootings, mistreatment
by police, political corruption, blatant discrimination, and nearly
everything having to do with government. In the words of many, *"The
country's going to hell, and no one seems to care."*

Political elections tap into the anger and distrust voters feel for
Washington. Most are convinced the system is rigged in favor of the
powerful and influential, and they believe politicians previously elected
to right these wrongs have only made them worse. In addition, voters
these days are more likely to vote *against* something rather than *for*
something. They vote against the establishment, the dysfunction of

government, and not least of all, against unpopular candidates who smile while telling endless half-truths.

Anger is a feeling of annoyance, displeasure, or hostility. It has at least a hundred synonyms; words that range from aggravated, livid, and outraged to irate, rabid, and vengeful. That's a lot of anger, no matter what you call it. But it's nothing new; history is replete with anger about competing ideas and beliefs. Behind this anger often lies an unconscious fear of "others", those perceived to be different from the rest of us. It is the response to every sad event from the crucifixion of Jesus to the medieval crusades, and it includes exploitation of Native Americans, racist nationalism in Germany in the 1930s, anti-communist McCarthy hearings of the 1950s, and resistance to civil rights legislation of the 1960s. *You're different from me; so please, do us both a favor and get lost!*

If you want an extreme—as well as extremely foolish—example of conflicting ideas consider the Sunni-Shia divide. It started the day after Prophet Mohammed died, more than 1,300 years ago! Shia believe that Mohammed's cousin Ali, who was the first-born Muslim, should be the leader after the Prophet's death. Sunni claimed that Abu Bakr, the prophet's closest and eldest confidante, should lead the Muslims.

These opinions have led to unending discord between Sunni and Shia and a perpetual conflict throughout the Middle East. Shias believe the religion should reflect contemporary life and needs. Sunnis argue that the religion should faithfully replicate the practices and behavior of the Prophet during his life. There are other differences, but consider this: both parties speak the same language, worship the same God, and both equally believe the word of the Quran. Yet they have been at each other's throats for centuries, and the animosity continues. Do you believe people should carry a grudge for 1300 years? Isn't there a statute of limitation that applies to anger and hate? If not, there certainly should be.

Actually, the Sunni-Shia rift is not that different from the many Southerners who have been distressed for over 150 years by the results of the U.S. Civil War. Many continue to display the Confederate flag and insist that secession from the Union over the issue of slavery was justified and necessary, even though more Americans died fighting other Americans than in both World Wars combined. Was the death of 620,000 young Americans really worth it?

In many ways modern life in America is better today than it has ever been. We are generally healthier and have consistently increased our life expectancy. But with every modern advantage comes irritations. The cell phone, for example, allows us to wander about while staying connected. But since elimination of the phone booth (remember those?) people now speak loudly on their phones in public, and all consideration for the privacy of others has vanished. You've probably heard a distracted grocery shopper speaking loudly, "Was that two quarts of milk and a loaf of bread or one milk and two breads?" And all you want to say is, "For Chrissake, get two of each and shut up already!"

Another frustration is the abundance of cars throughout every city. Every major street during rush hour is now pretty much an overcrowded parking lot. If you want to know what makes people angry, just drive crosstown in almost any city at about 5:30 one evening and listen to the honking horns and foul language. Even tuning in your car radio to the romantic music station is of little help.

The proliferation of Cable TV provides instant access to every worldwide catastrophe, atrocity, and injustice. Some may readily dismiss these events, but others will obsess over fears of what could possibly happen to *them* to upset their complacent way of life. TV also brings entertainment, but when shows based on extravagant lifestyles are paraded through our living rooms each night it becomes difficult to feel satisfied with our comparatively modest lives. In many cases, dissatisfaction leads to smoldering anger.

One may argue that original anger coincides with one's birth. Experts proclaim that infants under the age of six months experience unpleasant sensations that may resemble anger, but are not exactly the same as anger. I think the experts are wrong. Picture this: There you are, floating around in your private spa, amply fed, kept at a comfortable temperature, minding your own business, and having the time of your life. Suddenly, without warning, you're ejected into another world, a bright and cold world that lacks all the comforts you've grown to love and cherish. You hear loud voices, you're wrapped in constricting blankets, someone puts a silly hat on you, and ready or not, you're born. After all that, would you blame anyone for being annoyed, irritated, or genuinely outraged?

Frustration also arises in infants when their demands for attention—being fed or changed—are not immediately met. The process of becoming civilized, from early childhood on, makes some children rebellious and angry. What do you think a tantrum is all about, if not absolute, unadulterated anger?

Many wonder if anger is ever justified. In other words, do we ever have a right to get angry? The answer is absolutely yes. Anger has been a powerful tool for personal and social change as evidenced by the civil rights, feminist, anti-war, and other rights movements. Underlying each of these movements was a feeling of being unheard and ignored. Using anger effectively has essentially changed the course of history and has allowed humans of differing backgrounds and ideologies to coexist in peace.

On the other hand, you should be aware that your anger might just be a personal affront, such as becoming outraged when viewing someone wearing socks with flip-flops or a T-shirt with a profane message. You might also react with undue hostility to those with facial piercings, multiple tattoos, or hair dyed pink or green. Happily, it's a free country, and some may applaud as incredibly original that which offends others. Your response to such situations should avoid sarcastic comments, since the offending party may not get it, you might precipitate a battle, and I can absolutely guarantee you that nothing will change.

The real question is how should an angry person respond appropriately while remaining civil? If every person who felt anger reacted in rage there would be more death and destruction than in a full-scale war. The goal is to learn ways to express anger without causing the breakdown of relationships, self-destruction, or death. How many lives have been affected by road rage, when two irate drivers lose control and ultimately one gets stabbed, shot, or ends up with a concussion from a tire iron? Is a bent fender really worth all that?

Angry protests have often led to improved conditions; but when dissatisfaction turns to hostility, it is just as likely to be polarizing and destructive. Angry people are poor communicators, even worse listeners, and they often have trouble imagining other points of view. When both parties are angry, say goodbye to compromise. They'll be shouting past one another and any reasonable discussion will be out of the question.

Finally, if you are generally disillusioned, feel mistreated, and frustrated by the vicissitudes of your disappointing life, you are probably angry. Welcome to the club; so are most people, to one degree or another. But you should realize that the American Dream is still alive; this is a great country, where change is possible and lives can be improved. Optimism leads to hope, and hope remains a potent antidote to anger. On the other hand, if you're really at your wit's end, and have had it with the endless abuses of life, get up out of your chair. Like Howard Beale, get up right now and go to the window, open it, stick your head out and yell bloody murder. Maybe you'll feel better.

Frank Lloyd Wright

Frank Lloyd Wright is widely considered the greatest architect of the 20th century and the greatest American architect of all time. He was born in Wisconsin two years after the end of the Civil War and died nearly ninety-two years later at the beginning of the Space Age. He was a maverick, visionary crusader, and acknowledged genius. He was also a manipulator of facts. One of the most creative undertakings of his career was to present his life as he wished to be seen, regardless of the reality. For example, the early education Wright claimed was in sharp contrast to the facts. He never completed high school and later, spent perhaps one year, not the three he alleged, at the University of Wisconsin. At some point in his young life he also modified his date of birth by two years so as to appear more of a *wunderkind* than he was already considered. Two years? I mean, why bother?

Though generally recognized as a non-conformist, Wright's dramatic exploits continued to shock 19th and even 20th century sensibilities. His life became a scandalous soap opera long before there was such a thing as a soap opera. At the age of 22 he married 18-year-old Catherine Tobin, with whom he produced six children in the next thirteen years. While that sort of domestic situation might test the faith of any husband, the charming young architect was already considered hopelessly unfaithful. After twenty years of marriage he deserted Catherine and ran off with Mamah Cheney, the wife of a client for whom he was building a new home. The two went to Europe, set up housekeeping in Italy, and never looked back with regret.

When Wright and Cheney eventually returned to the United

States, Wright designed a home and studio for them on the land of his maternal ancestors in Spring Green, Wisconsin. Named Taliesin, Welsh for "shining brow", it was one of the most acclaimed works of his career. However, tragedy struck a year later when a deranged servant set fire to the house, burning it to the ground and axed to death Cheney and six others. Though Wright was devastated by the loss of his lover and home, he began at once to rebuild Taliesin in order to—in his own words—*"wipe the scar from the hill."*

Several years later Wright met and fell in love with Miriam Noel. Their marriage lasted less than a year after Noel became addicted to morphine. Wright was a non-smoker and teetotaler and was known to have little patience for those with addictions. The last of Wright's wives was Olgivanna Vanova Lazovich, a Montenegrin dancer. The two moved into Taliesin and were married shortly after Olga became pregnant with their daughter. The faithful Olga outlived her husband by sixteen years.

Frank Lloyd Wright was clearly a radical genius marching through life to his own drumbeat, and his unconventional behavior particularly extended to financial dealings. He had continuous self-inflicted money problems, as his tastes consistently ran miles ahead of his earnings. He lived by his often-stated rule: *"Give me the luxuries of life and I will willingly do without the necessities."* Wright habitually charmed advances out of clients, left a trail of unpaid bills, and almost every project exceeded its construction budget. He was frequently driven to bankruptcy and often sued by clients, workers, and others.

Needless to say, he was often in court, when, as a last resort, an injured party filed suit against him. In one famous instance, while being sworn in, he was asked by the court officer to state his full name and occupation.

"My name is Frank Lloyd Wright," he replied, "and I am the world's greatest architect."

"Really, Mr. Wright," admonished the judge, "is that sort of thing necessary?"

"Indeed it is, your honor," replied Wright, "Remember, I am under oath."

Frank Lloyd Wright

If the above paragraphs suggest that the arrogant architect was out of step with those around him, one must recall an earlier Wright pronouncement: *"Early in life, I had to choose between honest arrogance and hypocritical humility. I chose honest arrogance and have seen no occasion to change."*

More astonishing than Wright's attitude is that within a lifetime of unending turmoil there emerged one incredible piece of architecture after another. He once said, *"I just shake them out of my sleeve."* But it was not a magic sleeve; it was his prodigious talent.

Those who have never walked into a Frank Lloyd Wright building cannot appreciate the magnitude of his artistic skill. It is unlike any spatial experience you can imagine. Some great monuments of history, Notre Dame in Paris or St. Peter in Rome, for example, might replicate similar awe-inspiring charisma, but the designer of those spaces, talented though they were, could not wring out of a visitor the emotions produced so effortlessly by Wright.

Frank Lloyd Wright designed more than a thousand buildings during his lifetime, a third of which were produced during his last decade. The most accessible of his structures is one of the last of his career—the Solomon R. Guggenheim Museum on Fifth Avenue in New York. The building was completed six months after Wright's death, and remains today—almost sixty years later—an inspiring, architectural masterpiece.

Most art museums are palaces or pavilions where one circulates from one gallery to the next, but Wright created in the Guggenheim an unconventional circular spiral design that takes visitors by elevator to the top of the building and allows them to stroll down a continuous, gently sloping ramp while viewing the collection. A massive skylight at the center lights the interior, and the entire experience is uniquely different from any other art museum.

Wright developed the circular spiral theme years earlier for the V.C. Morris gift shop on Maiden Lane in San Francisco. That project was quite small and occupied a site along the narrow street of elegant shops. I was a graduate student in the Architectural Department at Berkeley during that time, and our Student Association thought it would be a wonderful experience to have Mr. Wright speak to us when he next visited the Bay Area to oversee the Morris project.

Our Association asked me to send an invitation to Mr. Wright. He answered my note saying he would be delighted, but his fee would be $250, which today would be more than ten times that amount. Since the balance in our Association's treasury was about twenty dollars, the proposed lecture appeared to be out of the question.

The German-born international architect, Eric Mendelsohn, who taught our graduate design class, was one of Mr. Wright's old friends. "I offered Wright a tour of our department", said Mendelsohn, "and he will be here this Friday." The famous architect arrived in Berkeley wearing his pork-pie hat, scarf, cloak, and walking stick, a genuine sight to behold. He was also considerably shorter in stature than I imagined. I thought that someone with such a monumental reputation, not to mention ego, would be much taller. I shook his hand, but remained nearly speechless with reverence.

"Sorry we couldn't get together," said Mr. Wright "Apparently we all have money problems. When you begin to practice you'll know what I mean."

Mendelsohn led Wright through the building while discussing the several projects on display for his visit. Meanwhile, they were trailed by a growing swarm of students. Then Wright walked into the brick-paved courtyard and sat on a bench, while students gathered around. He proceeded to give an hour-long lecture, at no fee whatever, consisting of his philosophy, mixed with severe criticism of formal education. "Architecture is doing, not listening to lectures," he said. "Stop wasting your time here; go out and build something, that's the only way you're going to learn anything." Upon leaving, Wright was heard to say, "I feel like crying for all these young, smiling students being so disillusioned." True to his advance publicity, Mr. Wright was arrogant, charming, and inspirational.

Over the years I have visited dozens of Frank Lloyd Wright buildings, and each was as inspiring as every other great monument I had ever seen, including the Pyramids of Egypt, the Gothic Cathedrals of France, and the unique Taj Mahal in India.

Frank Lloyd Wright

My most treasured visit was a journey several years ago to view Fallingwater, a weekend home for the Edgar Kaufmann family designed by Wright in 1935 in rural Pennsylvania. The home was built partly over a waterfall on Bear Run in the Allegheny Mountains. It is now a National Historic Landmark, having been judged by the American Institute of Architects as "best all-time work of American architecture".

After meeting the owner at Bear Run, Wright requested a survey, including the site's boulders, trees, and topography. Kaufmann called Wright several months later to announce that he would visit that day before lunch. He could not wait to see the plans for his new house. Wright had told Kaufmann he'd been working diligently on the plans, but in fact, he had not drawn a single line. After breakfast that morning, Wright sat down at his drawing board and calmly drew the plans in the two hours it took Kaufmann to arrive. He had apparently worked out every feature in his head, and the drawings flowed onto paper complete in every detail.

Though Kaufmann wanted the house located on the southern bank of Bear Run, directly facing the falls, Wright placed the home above the falls to afford a view of the cascades. Fallingwater stands as one of Wright's greatest masterpieces both for its dynamism and for its integration with the natural surroundings.

Walking through the spaces of Fallingwater is as close to a religious experience as one can imagine. Every proportion, relationship, and detail is perfectly realized. This is truly a *tour de force* of Wright's organic philosophy and a perfect example of harmony between man and nature. As Wright often said, *"Architecture should belong where you see it standing. It should be a grace to the landscape, not a disgrace."*

Frank Lloyd Wright left not only a fabulous legacy of buildings, but also a number of quotable thoughts, such as:

- *"The longer I live the more beautiful life becomes. If you foolishly ignore beauty, you will soon find yourself without it. Your life will be impoverished. But if you invest in beauty, it will remain with you all the days of your life."*

- *"A doctor can bury his mistakes, but an architect can only advise his clients to plant vines."*
- *"I'm all in favor of keeping dangerous weapons out of the hands of fools. Let's start with typewriters."*

Finally, an amusing and revealing incident about the great architect: "Wingspread" is the residence Wright designed in 1936 for the Herbert Johnson family. Shaped like a four-winged pinwheel, the large house is anchored by a thirty-foot high brick chimney surrounded on all sides by rows of skylights. To one side is the Great Hall that serves as the dining space.

Johnson insisted that the house be ready for occupancy by Thanksgiving, at which time twenty-four family members would inaugurate the new house over dinner. With superhuman effort the construction crew obliged, and the family gathered on a rainy Thanksgiving evening. After being seated one relative noticed that several individual skylights were dripping water directly onto the lengthy dining table.

Johnson immediately telephoned the famous architect to report his unhappiness. The response from Wright to Johnson was, "Move the table!"

One April many years ago I was representing an architectural office that was designing, with another firm, a new passenger terminal for the Port of Los Angeles. The project required numerous meetings at the other firm's downtown office to resolve the endless details. At lunchtime one day I was walking along a busy street and noticed the headline in a paper rack: "Famed Architect Frank Lloyd Wright Dead at the Age of 91".

I was shocked. Wright had been such a personal hero for so long I believed he was immortal. I stopped walking, and suddenly and involuntarily began to shed a few tears. A passerby stopped to ask, "Are you alright?"

"No," I replied. "A dear friend—who I barely knew—just died."

Work

Just about everyone in the world works for a living, but according to a recent Gallup poll, only 13% of people actually *enjoy* going to work. You hear right—just thirteen fortunate employees out of a random hundred look forward to getting out of bed each morning, leaving home, and doing a job. Gallup said 63% of workers are "not engaged" or "unmotivated", and another 24% are "actually disengaged" or truly unhappy. In other words, millions of people work in jobs they genuinely hate. How depressing is that?

The poll found that the happiest employees are those who look forward to work, feel energized performing their jobs, and show some pride and enthusiasm when discussing what they do for a living. Top among those, according to authorities, are the clergy and firefighters, while among the least happy workers are security guards and those in sales. So if you're not actually as cheerful as a firefighting priest what should you be doing? It's my opinion that if you're good at what you do, you will probably be deliriously happy doing whatever that is. If, for example, you're a Zamboni driver you're obviously in ice-hockey heaven driving that huge machine around the rink.

It's likely that most unhappy workers rarely considered what they wanted to do with their lives. That's the kind of soul-searching decision that often brings on a migraine, especially in those who haven't the faintest idea what kind of work will make them happy. First graders are often asked, "What do you want to be when you grow up?" That's a silly question to ask a little kid who knows almost nothing about life. Perhaps the child might respond, "an astronaut, ballerina, or a pirate", which will rarely raise an eyebrow. But if a six-year-old boy answered, "a sperm donor, sommelier, or a molecular oncologist, it's a good bet he might have come from another galaxy.

As you get older, the question of what to do with your life becomes more important. Ideally, everyone wants job security, adequate pay, stimulating work, and pride in the work they do; but how are you supposed to follow your passion when you have no idea what that passion is? A Stanford Center study revealed that only 20% of young people have a clear goal of what they want to do with their lives. The other 80% may wander around trying different jobs, while hoping a fascinating job will just fall into their lap. Or as Scarlett O'Hara famously said, *"I'll think about it tomorrow."*

Here's a suggestion: Ask yourself what are you good at doing, what activities make you happy, and what did you love to do as a child? Maybe it was playing the clarinet, maybe painting pictures, perhaps creating new fashions for your dolls, or even telling jokes. Among those answers might be a clue. On the other hand, some may never find their passion, and those are the ones who make up the majority of unhappy workers. A young acquaintance once confessed, "All I want is a job where I can carry a leather briefcase." Obviously, it wasn't the job; it was the image. He ended up being a pest control supervisor who was never seen on the job without his tool kit and a spiffy leather briefcase, which probably contained nothing more than a license to exterminate termites, and perhaps his lunch.

Ogden Nash once suggested that people who work sitting down are paid more than those who work standing up. I suppose the implication is that accountants earn more than carpenters, but he said nothing about them being any happier. A more accurate distinction might be that using you brain generally gets you further in life than using your brawn, and unless you're a linebacker in the NFL that should certainly make you feel better.

Everyone loves to do what he or she is good at doing. If you are truly unhappy in your job, consider what might bring a happier life, quit your unfulfilling job, and work for yourself. There's always a chance you'll end up destitute, but on the other hand you might become a successful consultant, open a bookstore, write the great American play, or perhaps sell homemade cupcakes. It's your life, and with the infinite possibilities out there, why not take a shot at something different?

Years ago there were plenty of jobs available for youngsters, jobs that would teach them a few things about how the world actually worked. Those days are pretty much gone, and fewer of today's young people get experience working and getting paid for it. As a result, they know less about taking responsibility, getting along with co-workers, and managing whatever money they earn.

My first job came along when I was twelve years old. My dentist asked if I'd be interested in baby-sitting. His baby was a well-behaved three-year-old, and it turned out to be the easiest money I ever earned. Only once did I fall asleep on the job, and that was because the dentist had a flat tire and returned home two hours late.

When I was sixteen I got an after-school job working as a kitchen helper at McGregor's Modern Foods. I worked each day from four to seven o'clock and then bicycled home to have dinner and do homework. Chef McGregor was an early proponent of health food, and every entrée on the menu was accompanied by a choice of three vegetables. My job was to wash, peel, and slice the raw vegetables. The job paid very well, and because I was a bit compulsive, I was good at it. I realized, however, that if most able-bodied men were not off fighting a war, I probably never would have become a vegetable whiz kid.

The war provided other opportunities that might have gone to older workers, if they were available, but my résumé grew substantially as the months passed. I had a weekend job as an ice-skating guard at a local rink. My work consisted in skating backwards, while keeping speeders from creating havoc, and the bonus was wearing a bright red sweater and having a shrill whistle that I blew to my heart's content. I also set pins in a bowling alley before technology made that work obsolete and no career-ending injury came my way. When every Japanese gardener was sent to internment camps during the war I began to cut lawns and trim hedges, which was difficult work, but profitable. At the age of seventeen I washed cars by hand one summer at the first automated car wash in town. The work was grueling, as the assembly line never stopped, but my bank account, as well as every muscle in my body, grew exponentially. Finally, after my graduation from high school I worked for a summer as a messenger at the RKO Studio in Hollywood. It was more fascinating than any previous job, as I watched great movies being made, met wonderfully creative people, and was sad to see it end.

So what's the point of reviewing every odd job of my young life? Just this: All jobs have much in common. To begin with, one learns responsibility. Woody Allen said, *"Eighty percent of success is showing up."* I would add, "showing up on time", which demonstrates *real* responsibility. One also learns to get along with coworkers, take directions, and understand that all actions, good and bad, have consequences. They say that nothing you learn is ever wasted. I would add that nothing you experience is ever wasted as well; it continues to influence all that follows.

Employment is an agreement between employer and employee; you do what the job requires, and the employer pays you regularly and on time. If either one of you fails to hold up his or her end of the bargain, you have a problem. It certainly helps if you tackle your work with more smiles than frowns. No one likes to be around grouchy workers, so you should get along with others the way you were taught in kindergarten. Some believe that the camaraderie in a working group is actually the most satisfying part of a job. Relationships develop, and the workplace becomes a second home.

Research shows that workplaces are where the majority of couples meet. Unlike online dating, newspaper ads, or meddling relatives, the office allows you to know and bond with limited personal commitment. Working side by side with someone daily, seeing him or her under pressure, empathizing over problems and celebrating wins gives you a view of the person that would be hard to replicate under other circumstances. Such relationships develop in a natural fashion and are often long lasting, because they're based on reality. Unfortunately, the same ingredients can make personal office connections tempting, even to married workers, which can create awkward situations.

Many people date in the workplace, though it may be dangerous, because it's so easy to meet and get to know someone well. Coworkers often share personal information, engage in long talks, and sometimes lunch together. After a while you may want to spend more time with your coworker out of the office, and that's when the relationship may reach another level. It may become serious and loving, or it could bring you to the edge of the cliff. And so our fictional coworkers may end up blissfully happy, or with either one or both out of a job.

My own lifelong profession—architecture—appeared fairly late in life. A high school friend knew he would be an attorney at the age of twelve, and another was a writer before the age of seventeen. I, on the other hand, was seriously adrift when I began college at the age of eighteen.

"What did you study in high school," asked my advisor?

"I had few years of math," I replied, "and I did okay."

"Well then, let's say math will be your major," said the advisor.

And just like that my questionable future was decided. I became a reluctant math major. What a catastrophe that turned out to be! I hated every class I took, lasted exactly one semester, and became a depressed dropout. Although I was proud to be the first person in my family to attend college, I was also the first to drop out. I swore I would never return to any college anywhere, ever.

Two years later I was invited by friends to attend a football weekend at the University of California in Berkeley. I had been home a few months after spending a year on a rusty tanker as an itinerant seaman. I had exciting adventures and wonderful memories but was no closer to finding my place in life. I was sure of only two things: I would never become a professional sailor or a depressed, second-rate mathematician. One of my friends was enrolled in the Department of Architecture and during that weekend he gave me a tour of the place. I met a few students, viewed attractive drawings and models, and suddenly knew this is where I belonged. Like the classic light bulb over the head moment, I suddenly knew this was something I really wanted to do.

I remembered the pleasure of a mechanical drawing class in high school and I recalled my instructor suggesting I might want to consider architecture as a profession. But what fifteen-year-old takes such advice seriously? In retrospect I think everything I'd always enjoyed led me to this profession. My mother actually wrote in my Baby Book: *From the time he held a pencil he was content to sit on the floor and doodle images of houses, trees, and animals.* And that was when I was about four years old! I also loved playing with building blocks and Lincoln Logs. During my teens I built and flew model airplanes and later designed them. Since everything pointed to my ultimate profession, why had my future been such a perpetual mystery? As they say, "That's life."

I believe there's an element of luck in all you do. Some don't believe there is such a thing as luck; they claim you make your own luck. Others, some years ago, carried a rabbit's foot for luck, while skeptics claimed, "It obviously didn't bring much luck to the rabbit." So what's the deal? You can work hard, be prepared, live an exemplary life, and still get dealt a two or three card to go along with the ace in your hand. While the guy next to you, also with an ace, pulls a face card every time and ends up with a blackjack fortune. If that isn't luck, you'll never convince the winner—or the loser.

Finding one's life's work is easy for some; often it's as simple as adding *"and son"* to you Father's business card. At other times you're forced, through an evolutionary process, to eliminate the meaningless jobs you thought would bring you endless pleasure together with riches beyond your dreams. If you're lucky, and it all works out in the end, the dream may become a reality, and you will bless the day you discovered the work you were born to do.

Travel

Why are you sitting there? Turn off the TV, put on your traveling shoes and get going. Somewhere. Anywhere. There's a whole world to explore, and no time to lose. Don't wait for the Golden Years; for all you know, you may never reach them. Go now, hop on a plane, board a train, go somewhere special; and if your partner disagrees, go alone. Remember what the great traveler, Mark Twain said: *"Years from now you'll be more disappointed by the things you didn't do, then the things you did do."*

Travel is a rewarding adventure, uniquely enlightening, and the source of endless memories. As such, it is especially valuable for young people. And that's why more youths than ever are taking time off from school these days or leaving their unfulfilling jobs to hit the road. It's the best time in one's life to take a chance, open your mind to new thoughts, and explore foreign cultures head on. So live a little.

Since the beginning of time people have been on the move. First were the nomadic hunters who wandered in search of food. Later came development of the wheel and crude rafts, both designed to move people with less effort. Early Christian pilgrims and missionaries enthusiastically took to the road to evangelize so-called heathens and spread the word of their new religion.

You might also recall the exciting stories of early heroes from the great Age of Exploration. Marco Polo, a 13th century traveler, spent four years traveling by boat, horse, camel, and on foot to reach China. During the 15th century other brave souls searched for a direct route to the treasures of the Far East. The most famous of these was Christopher Columbus, who believed he was in Asia after landing in the Bahamas. Amerigo

Vespucci arrived a bit later, explored nearby areas, and ultimately, the Latin equivalent of his first name—Americus—was applied to the actual place they both landed—America.

One can hardly appreciate the courage and determination it took for an explorer to exchange a comfortable life for the dubious goal of discovering new and exciting foreign lands. The earliest men set sail into the unknown, with no charts to guide them, searching for adventure, wealth, and glory. Some believed the world was flat, and at any moment they might fall off the edge. What kind of person abandons a familiar life and risks mortal danger to be part of a precarious future? The slightly deranged, of course, but more likely the adventurous sort that envisions the excitement and rewards of the largely unknown. Early travelers were genuine heroes, who helped define the world we know today.

When Thomas Jefferson, our third president, purchased the Louisiana Territory from the French in 1803, he doubled the size of our country and prompted the great westward expansion. Seizing the opportunity for land ownership and economic freedom, families moved west in covered wagons with the same fortitude as earlier explorers. The trails they blazed established the highway system that appeared a hundred years later.

The emerging Industrial Revolution produced the railroad, and with it, the ability to travel comfortably at previously unimaginable speeds. Transcontinental travel was suddenly cut from four months to four days! After World War II air travel became popular and soon gave rise to the jet age. For the first time a direct coast-to-coast trip took only hours. Every advance in transportation development led to greater leisure travel, and most people today hop on a plane as easily one might have jumped aboard a streetcar several years ago. Just think, these days you can leave Los Angeles after lunch and have breakfast in Beijing the next morning. What would Marco Polo think of that?

My own travels began many years ago when our family moved from Chicago to Los Angeles. It was hardly my idea, as nine-year-olds in those days were rarely consulted about things like that. My father and his brother-in-law decided to open an office in a new area, and that included moving both families. Our caravan of cars followed the most direct highway of the day, Route 66. If you're familiar with the lyrics of the famous song by Bobby Troupe you know every highlight of that trip.

If you ever plan to motor west,
Travel my way, take the highway that's best.
Get your kicks on Route sixty-six.

The fact that this corny song became so popular remains one of life's unsolved mysteries. But trust me, as undistinguished as it was, it was infinitely more exciting than the actual ten-day ordeal. And for a little kid, who unfortunately got few kicks from Route 66, it was painfully boring. Oh sure, seeing the Rockies and real Indians was fine, and spending nights in strange motels was kind of interesting, but overall, it was about as exciting as watching someone cut an acre of lawn with a pair of scissors. If travel is really this disagreeable, I thought, it's something I can happily live without.

As a teenager, I read a book that changed that opinion and in many ways, my life. *The Royal Road to Romance* by Richard Halliburton was the author's account of his worldwide travels after graduating from Princeton. Halliburton chose adventure as his career, and he spent years traveling from one thrilling exploit to the next. In his search for excitement and romance, Halliburton climbed the Matterhorn, swam the Hellespont, hunted tigers in India, bathed in the Nile, scaled Mount Fujiyama, and took a dip in the Taj Mahal pool, among his many other adventures. His charm and exuberance was inspirational, and I fell for it all. He aroused in me an irresistible passion to travel and explore, and I've been doing that ever since.

After an unhappy semester of college, I dropped out and became a merchant seaman. For most of the following year I traveled on a tanker from wherever oil was produced to wherever it was needed. We headed for the Persian Gulf and passed through the Suez Canal a half dozen times, while delivering oil throughout Europe. We also loaded oil in Venezuela and delivered it to other South American ports. I became a seaman at the age of eighteen, and after nearly a year I returned to the U.S. feeling like a mature adult.

It is said of any trip, if you are lucky you will not be the same person when you return. That was certainly true for me. All travel is an adventure, a challenge, and an education. And wherever you go your trip will be like no one else's. It will reward you with unforgettable and unique personal experiences.

After completing my education I won a travelling fellowship that enabled me to spend the next year seeing the sights of Europe, Near East, and North Africa. Since those exciting days I have continued to travel and visit new places and old favorites. Travel has never lost its appeal, and I believe new experiences are just around the corner for us all.

Travel these days differs from the way it was years ago. Everyone is on the move today, airports are jam-packed, security is a major issue, and travel is more work, less special, and hardly the fun it once was. On a DC-3 flight long ago from Chicago to New York every man wore a suit and tie. On my last flight from Cabo San Lucas to Los Angeles everyone looked as though they were still at the beach; T-shirts, shorts, and flip-flops were the prevailing uniform. Casual dress is more acceptable than ever these days, but few realize, that your appearance often dictates how airline personnel, not to mention fellow passengers, treat you.

Another reason that travel is different these days is that the Internet has made everyone a minor expert in nearly everything. Having seen and done too much already, many have become jaded and simply lack interest. So what does it take to amaze and thrill travelers these days? Obviously, much more than what the following disappointed travelers reported in a recent survey.

- The Grand Canyon – *"It's nothing special; not worth a nine-hour drive."*
- The Eiffel Tower – *"More like the Awful Tower. Views okay—if you like views,"*
- Coliseum in Rome – *"There's actually nothing on the inside."*

- Stonehenge – "It's just a pile of rocks. A complete waste of time."
- Great Pyramids – *People on camels harassing you for money. Bad experience."*

The origin of the word "travel" comes from an Anglo-French word meaning "travail". That indicates travel was once considered a torment of painful and arduous nature. That was mostly true when one journeyed anywhere during the Middle Ages. You should realize that travel was rarely faster than the pace of a tired horse, and rest rooms at service stations, as well as roadside fast food, were hundreds of years in the future. Travel today can still be a pain when your pocket is picked in Barcelona, rats appear in your New Delhi hotel room, or you change money at a sidewalk Cambia in Italy, whose rate of exchange turns out to be higher than the Burj Khalifa in Dubai. Yes, travel can be–and often is–challenging.

A word about packing: It has been suggested by many travellers that prior to leaving home you should lay out all the clothes you plan to take, as well as the money you have budgeted for your trip. Now remove half the clothes and double the amount of money. Most will ignore this advice, because it sounds constraining. "What if I want to wear tennis shoes?" one may ask. "I'm only taking four pair of shoes as it is".

Many people go about packing in the most irrational way; they take nearly every article of clothing they own, pack them in as many pieces of luggage as necessary, and upon arrival decide the appropriate outfit to wear day by day. The more reasonable approach would be to decide what to wear each day and then pack only those particular clothes, preferably in one compact bag. A dose of reality: You will not horrify foreigners if you appear in the same outfit two days in a row. Don't be offended, but it's unlikely they will even notice.

Let me reveal a true story about deprivation and survival. As a student years ago, my rucksack was stolen from a youth hostel in Cologne. I was writing a letter at the time, and the only possessions that remained were the suit I was wearing, my wallet with passport and money, and a change of underwear I had just laundered. The next morning I purchased a new comb, toothbrush, toothpaste, and a container for them and my change of underwear. The container was a child's pencil box, the contents of which I gave away, except for the pencil. I traveled through Germany for the next two weeks with my one suit, shirt, and tie, and of course, my pencil box. I was never refused service anywhere, nor was I shunned by anyone who probably assumed my luggage was in storage. I eventually replaced my lost clothes in Munich, but for two weeks I was free from the burden of luggage, unperturbed about what I would wear each morning, and gratified that no one treated me as though I were inappropriately dressed. The experience was extraordinarily liberating. I do not suggest you do the same, but on the other hand, why not consider it? Incidentally, in the Alfred Hitchcock film, *North by Northwest,* Cary Grant wore the very same suit in every exciting scene, over a period of several days, and looked better than any of us will ever look, *ever!*

There is a common paradox at the airport, that some of you may have noticed. Quite often the worst dressed passengers check in with the largest pieces of luggage. What could possibly be in those steamer trunks? More mismatched clothes? A suit of armor? A waffle iron?

I never, ever, check luggage, regardless of the length of the trip. If it doesn't fit in the overhead compartment I leave it home. Consequently, I never pay a baggage fee, wait at a crowded carousel, experience a lost or damaged bag, or are my possessions ever out of my control. Many think that's a silly way to travel, but as the seasoned traveler, Antoine de Saint-Exupéry, author of the "Little Prince", once said, *"He who travels happily must travel light."*

Go argue with *him.*

Fear

Alfred Hitchcock was a film writer, director, and producer, who was often referred to as "The Master of Suspense". He pioneered many elements of psychological terror and unmitigated fear among the 65 films he directed, including *Vertigo, The Birds,* and *Psycho.* Each film fulfilled Hitchcock's core belief: *"Always make the audience suffer as much as possible."* And suffer they did. For example, Psycho's vicious knifing-in-the-shower scene had hysterical audiences running up and down the aisles; and the sound of screams in the auditorium were so deafening, few could hear the famous soundtrack of frenzied violins. If you were not terrified watching human blood circle the shower drain, you were napping, or possibly drugged. As a result of those fearsome images, thousands of moviegoers avoided daily showers months after the movie made its debut.

From King Kong holding the hysterical Faye Wray to the great white shark in *Jaws,* movie audiences have been wetting their pants in fear, while enjoying every tense moment of horror movies. Just the thought of a Freddy Krueger or Hannibal Lecter can cause sweaty palms and elevated blood pressure. Apparently, being scared out of one's wits is not only exhilarating, but the adrenaline rush provides incomparable entertainment for many thrill-seeking audiences.

Horror movies provide an opportunity for us to confront our fears, but since we realize it's just a movie, we don't have to face reality. Stephen King, the famous creator of horror stories, compared scary films to a roller coaster ride. *"We seek out the experience to prove we are not afraid. Frightening movies deliberately appeal to the worst in us. They free our base instincts and allow our most wicked fantasies to be realized. For better or worse, all this happens in the dark".*

Fear is the unpleasant emotion caused by the belief that someone or something is a dangerous threat and likely to cause us trouble, or worse yet, unbearable pain. We may be born with certain fears, but most are learned through experience. Since the beginning of civilization, the positive aspect of fear has afforded us protection from potential danger. If you feared wild animals, for example, chances are you knew to flee before being attacked by a saber-toothed tiger. And fear of lakes and streams prevented drowning, while fearless non-swimmers got in over their heads and were never heard from again.

Two more popular phobias, agoraphobia and claustrophobia, which are fears of open and closed spaces, also developed during prehistoric times. Walking across an open field made you a target of wild animals, while being trapped in a cave—with no means of escape—could result in a painful death caused by wandering wolves. Agoraphobics these days are uncomfortable walking down empty streets at night, while claustrophobics prefer an aisle seat in the theater, and may even feel uncomfortable during a short elevator ride.

When prehistoric people were confronted with a dangerous sight, sound, or other perceived threat; hormonal reactions produced what is called the fight-or-flight response. There was an increased heart rate, blood flow, and rapid breathing that prepared the threatened person to throw a spear or run like crazy to survive. Today, those same hormonal responses are triggered by far less critical events. If you are anxious being late to a meeting, forgetting your homework, or receiving a threatening letter from the IRS, fight or flight serves little purpose. Any number of situations can make your heart beat faster, but who do you fight, or in what direction do you run? So you reduce the anxiety with a tranquilizer or possibly a soothing cocktail. We should all be much happier realizing how far we've come from the time when we might have thrown a spear or been forced to bolt like a terrified rabbit.

Fear begins early in life, and it is perfectly normal that all children become fearful at some point in their childhood. Newborns fear being separated from those who feed and protect them, because an infantile mind may ask, "What if those people never come back?" Loud noises create other fears that overload delicate senses. A vacuum cleaner, popped balloon, or even a distant siren can set off a child's endless wailing.

Strangers represent yet another childish fear. Children recognize at once the difference between their parents and the rest of the world, because of their looks, sound of voices, and because of what parents mean to them. Worse yet is a stranger in costume, like a clown or even a Santa Claus. Now the kid is thinking, "Who is this fat guy with a white beard and dressed in a red suit? I've never seen him before, and I'm supposed to sit on his lap? No thanks; I'll skip it, if you don't mind. And the same goes for the guy in a rabbit suit carrying a basket of chocolate eggs. Maybe another time—or maybe never."

When we think back to our childhood, those glorious days of irresponsibility and endless playtime, we often forget how frightening life could sometimes be. If you grew up with Grimm's Fairy Tales, as I did, you learned about good people and bad, but it was the dangerous ogres, the wicked stepmothers, the evil witches, and the endless dangers faced by innocent protagonists that kept you up nights. And if it wasn't that, it was the crocodile living under your bed that ruined many a good night's sleep. One false move and suddenly you'd be sporting nine toes instead of ten! Even a family movie, like "The Wizard of Oz" had a frightening, wicked witch along with a terrifying army of flying monkeys. With time and experience we eventually discovered that things that seemed scary weren't so scary after all. We also began to realize our remarkable capacity to manage our fears.

We live these days in one of the most peaceful and healthful times in history. Yet many walk around with anxiety and fear. Fear of what, you may ask? Just about anything from nuclear war to finding lost car keys. We all fear something—every single one of us. Some still fear the dark, others are afraid of heights, spiders, germs, snakes, and not least of all, death. Fear still keeps people out of airplanes, even though the odds of dying in an auto accident are nearly fifteen times more likely than in a plane.

John Madden, the successful coach of the Oakland Raiders, flew until 1979, when he had a sudden and severe panic attack during a short flight. He explained that the panic had nothing to do with flying or heights, but rather with claustrophobia. From that moment on Madden never again stepped inside an airplane. He traveled from game to game in his personal, customized bus, often coast to coast several times a season. So whether it's claustrophobia, aerophobia, or any one of the dozens of other phobias, fear controls the way we live to greater extent than most care to admit.

There are anxious people around us that fear everything from people who don't look exactly like them to the potential problems tomorrow may bring. Several lists of top-ten fears cover broad subjects like Crime (murder, rape, theft), Natural Disasters (earthquakes, hurricanes, floods), Government (corruption, taxes), and Personal Anxiety (lack of money, public speaking). As you probably realize, there is no shortage of phobias that can raise our blood pressure. The humorist, Robert Benchley once facetiously said, "Tell us your phobias and we'll tell you what you're afraid of". Unfortunately, phobias usually sound worse than the fear they identify. For example, many men fear going bald, but if you called them "phalacrophobics" they might feel even worse.

I first learned of phobias years ago when my father called my mother a "lackapetrophobic". Here's the story: My father had an odd habit of avoiding gas stations until the gas gauge arrow hovered over the bright red "E", standing for empty. This drove my mother crazy, as she saw little reason to tempt fate and possibly end up at the side of some lonely road, out of gas and out of luck. My father, on the other hand, when challenged would say, "Not to worry, we've enough gas to drive to Pomona and back." I don't know where that came from, because Pomona was 40 miles away, but no one in our family had ever been there. Nevertheless, my mother continued to fear the worst until my father finally labeled her fear neurotic.

"You're developing an irrational case of lackapetrophobia," he said.

"What's that?" we all wanted to know.

"Fear of running out of gas," he answered.

"You just made that up," claimed my mother.

Years later I discovered that mother—as usual—was right, but I always admired my father's resourcefulness and ingenuity, as well as his incredible luck of never running out of gas.

All fears are warnings of potential danger. Although some fears are neurotic, like fearing tigers that you're never likely to encounter in the middle of a city; other fears are practical, like running out of money, which can be more frightening than a tiger on the loose. Other practical fears are being caught in bed with someone not your spouse, being trapped into lying about it, suffering humiliation, getting sued for divorce, and finally, losing your spouse, your job, most friends, and what's left of your reputation.

Glossophobia is the fear of public speaking, or of speaking in general. A great many people consider this phobia the worst possible affliction, and the intense anxiety it produces may cause nausea, ulcers, and cardiovascular damage. We're not just talking about stage fright here, but rather extreme physical and mental discomfort. It has been estimated that seventy-five percent of all people experience some degree of anxiety when speaking in public. In fact, surveys have shown that many people fear public speaking more than they fear death. Really? As impossible as that is to believe, some would rather die than say a few words in public, which makes you realize how severe some fears can be.

Like most fears, the fear of public speaking begins early in life, often because of a traumatic experience. Perhaps the reluctant speaker was ridiculed or even booed off the stage in some elementary school play. Regardless, the fear is real, and one often spends an entire lifetime avoiding any risky situation that ends up on center stage being humiliated and looking foolish. Oddly, politicians who give speeches at the drop of a hat have no such reluctance to speak publicly, regardless of the outcome. In fact, some politicians have few fears at all, including manipulating the truth, flip-flopping, and acting like egotistical bullies.

Many people claim that fears can be easily conquered if we would just put mind over matter, so to speak. Dale Carnegie, the self-improvement expert, said, *"Fear doesn't exist anywhere, except in the mind."* Obviously, Dale was never bitten on the ass by an angry pit bull; otherwise he might have had reconsidered his arrogance. The author, Napoleon Hill agreed that, *"Fear is nothing more than a state of mind,"* but one wonders how Hill would react if someone pointed a gun at him and said, "Your money or your life?" Do you suppose the threat of death would be treated as simply a "state of mind?" Or would he likely open his wallet with trembling hands as he involuntarily wet his pants?

One of the most quoted views about fear was included in the first inaugural address of Franklin Delano Roosevelt in 1933. With the Great Depression reaching its depths and citizens suffering from personal depressions of their own, Roosevelt said, *"The only thing we have to fear is fear itself."* Roosevelt was essentially saying that fear, as well as inaction was preventing the country from solving its economic problems, and that such pessimism was unwarranted. His optimistic message of hope helped revive the economy and ultimately turned a critical situation into one of prosperity.

Among other famous advice about fear is the following notion of Mark Twain; *"If you do the thing you fear the most, the death of fear is certain."* I can't help wondering, however, about someone whose greatest terror is the fear of drowning. Can you imagine how counterproductive– to say the least–that might be? I'm sure Twain was trying to encourage people to overcome their fears by facing them head on, but jumping into a pool without actually knowing how to swim could very well be suicidal. Anyone taking Twain's suggestion literally is liable to end up more frightened than ever, if not a tragically disappointed, water-soaked corpse.

No less than the wisdom of the Holy Bible says, *"Be not afraid"* more than 350 times. Obviously, there was an awful lot of fear in those days, some of which may have impeded progress. Those same fears, however, helped keep civilization safe since the beginning of time.

So let's not all rush to become the most fearless trooper in history. Keep on trucking, as they say, but keep an eye out for lightening bolts, rabid pit bulls, and crazy drivers.

Friendship

If you're ever in a jam, here I am.
If you're ever in a mess, S.O.S.
It's friendship, friendship, just a perfect blendship.
When other friendships are soon forgot, ours will still be hot.

As the Cole Porter lyrics suggest, a friend is someone you can count on. In Porter's words, *"If you're ever down a well, ring my bell"*, means that you can often call a friend for help, because that's what friends are for. Friendship, however, is more than just responding to an emergency. It's a mutual affection between two people. It's someone to chat with, to depend on, and most of all, someone with whom you can be your true self as you share the joys and woes of life. The uniqueness of friendship is that it's voluntary; friends are friends because they choose to be. The family you were born into, on the other hand, often includes people you're more or less stuck with. You're never stuck with a friend in the same way, because if the relationship goes off the tracks, you simply stop seeing each other and hope for better luck next time.

Friendship is characterized by companionship and shared activities. It has no formal requirements or legal obligations, since the nature of friends is to provide emotional support and share intimate details without fear of embarrassment or harmful consequences. Another special quality of friendship is the informality. It might be difficult to ignore your spouse for a month or two, but you could go that long without contacting someone who remains a friend forever.

By the age of three or four, children often play together, share toys, and mutually enjoy activities that lead to early friendships. My first friend was a young neighbor by the name of David. I assume he had a last name, but to this day I have no idea what it was. I don't remember much more than the times we spent playing in a sand box with toy trucks. As you may know, little boys and toy trucks go together like macaroni and cheese. David and I loaded sand in our trucks, made a couple of "vroom, vroom" sounds, and dumped the sand elsewhere. It was a pretty trivial activity, but those happy days with my earliest friend remain a fond memory.

During middle childhood, we value a friend's loyalty and trust, while sharing personal secrets and thoughts. We also giggle over the same silly things. By the time you're in high school lifelong friendships often develop. That was my good fortune, and at the age of fourteen I became part of a small, like-minded group—actually three other boys—who were bright, charming, and incredibly funny. My memories of going to movies, the beach, or a hike in the mountains still generate a mental smile, as every adventure was filled with silliness and laughter. We truly loved being together, as we still do on rare occasions.

Being in high school is also the time one begins to consider potential friendships with the opposite sex. But since the emphasis is more on sex than friendship, you're lucky if you score on either one or the other. Nevertheless, the awkward fumbles of early romance served to provide my social group with humorous, tasteless, and almost endless taunting.

College is an environment like no other in facilitating friendships. Not only are you thrown together with others with similar interests and goals, but you may also be sharing rooms and meals with the same people. College relationships, like those in high school, can result in lifelong friends, not to mention romances. During my college years I roomed off-campus with two other architecture students. Both were talented and personable, but we came from different backgrounds, beliefs, and geographic areas. We got along well, sharing many of the same academic interests, but after graduation one roommate remained in touch for several years, while the other one disappeared faster than Halley's comet. That roommate and I had spent years speaking to each other every single day, but after graduation we never again exchanged a word. Unfortunately, that kind of loss is just one of the risks of friendship.

If you are a friendly person, you will likely continue developing friendships as life goes on. Co-workers often become close, as one is drawn to those with shared employment interests, and companionships develop during meetings, holiday celebrations, or simply exchanging small talk around the water cooler. Those, on the other hand, who have always been uncomfortable making new friends, might have a more difficult time, even among co-workers.

It is generally assumed that everyone has friends, but that's not actually the case. Most people are in touch with several others, but the others may be casual acquaintances, not real friends. It's estimated that perhaps a quarter of all people feel some sense of loneliness much of the time. They have no one to confide in, are socially isolated, and crave true friendships. Many of these people turn to social media sites like Twitter or Facebook, where they spend hours sharing information, opinions, and photos; while this activity becomes their concept of friendship. Many have hundreds of Facebook "friends", and despite a total lack of privacy, they reveal their most private thoughts that might better remain private. No doubt social media enables many to feel a genuine connection to others, but recent studies show that, for some, increased use of Facebook may lead to a less healthy and more isolated life. How can one possibly believe that staring at a computer screen offers the same affection and companionship that one gets by sitting face to face having a cup of coffee with a real pal?

The true impact of loneliness usually hits people after graduation. While at school you're with those of the same age and interests, and you see each other consistently over a long period. These are factors that encourage strong friendships. After leaving school, some move to new cities and jobs, while others get married and start families. Good for them, you think, but since their days are now filled with different interests, it's not always a suitable time for old friendships.

Before television, and even before that, people lived a simpler and friendlier kind of life.

You grew up and stayed in the same town, held the same job for years, everyone knew everybody else, and they helped each other when the need arose. Loneliness wasn't an issue in those days because most knew, on a first-name basis, their neighbors as well as their grocer, butcher, and service station attendant who pumped their gas. In fact, neighbors were often the best of friends. They would have coffee together, frequently share barbeques or dinners, and could be counted on to water the plants or feed the dog when you were away.

Do you even know your neighbors today? According to 2015 General Social Survey data, only about twenty percent of Americans say they spend time with neighbors, and nearly a third of the population reports no interaction whatsoever with people who live nearby. Contrast that with the way things were back in the 1970s, when nearly thirty percent of Americans reported hanging out with neighbors at least twice a week. So what happened? Essentially, the time we used to invest in neighborly relations is now spent watching television, texting everybody we barely know, and playing video games. Yes, technology has been good for society in some respects, but fairly disruptive in other ways. We are becoming so socially isolated many no longer feel the need to depend on neighbors as we did in the past.

Some people have moved to suburbs, where living has become even more private. There's been a surge in gated communities, which were designed to provide safety by keeping out most others. Sadly, Americans are growing further apart and talking less to people with differing opinions. In the past you might have ignored your neighbor's wrongheaded rants, but at least you recognized there was another legitimate point of view. What's going on in Washington these days is simply an extension of what's going on in neighborhoods. People aren't speaking to one another, nor have they much respect for other opinions. In fact, politicians new to Washington are advised–if they need a friend–to get a dog.

So how do we stop this spiral of unfriendliness–this decent into loneliness and indifference? Or do you really care? Some say, "I've got enough people in my life, so go peddle your friendliness elsewhere." Most others, however, agree we should make more friends–real friends. When my mother grew older she often complained that all her old friends were dying. She never lacked friendships previously, but now she began to feel isolated and abandoned. "What you need," I suggested, "are *younger* friends." She soon volunteered as an aide at a local hospital twice a week and spent another two days donating time at a thrift shop. Through both activities she met dozens of new, and mostly younger people, some of whom became close and loyal friends. In other words, you have to make a genuine effort if you want to improve your life.

They say that to make friends you must be friendly. Sounds reasonable, but there are certain emotions that may make that difficult. Perhaps you're shy, maybe you're a bit short on self-esteem, or possibly you feel the potential rejection is simply not worth the effort, and most people are jerks anyway. Well, just remember this: Humans are social creatures; we're not meant to be isolated from one another. Evidence shows that people with close friends live longer and are happier than those who are friendless. Friendship defines what it means to be human. The Greek philosopher Epicurus observed: "*Of all the things that help one live a happy life, the greatest by far is the possession of friends. Eating or drinking without a friend is only suitable for wild animals.*"

During my teenage years, I was a member of the Boy Scouts of America. I loved the experience, including wearing a uniform, camping out, and the many things I learned that serve me well today, like tying a square knot, for example. The Scout Law encouraged one to be– among other things–Trustworthy, Loyal, Helpful, Friendly, Courteous, and Kind. Now who can argue with that? Scouts were the original do-gooders, and held in the highest esteem was displaying public acts of kindness to random strangers. It became a familiar joke that when a scout saw a frail old lady standing at the side of the road, he'd inevitably help her get to the other side, often without asking if she really *wanted* to be on the other side. Sometimes, this ended with the old lady complaining that she didn't want to cross the street in the first place, and in the second place, please mind your own business. In some versions of the event, the old lady completed her scolding by whacking the scout with her oversized handbag.

I never had the opportunity to help a little old lady cross a street, but I had a similar experience several years ago that brings that situation to mind. I was walking along a busy city street when I noticed an old man standing on the dividing line between two lanes of traffic on each side whizzing by in opposite directions. The old man carried a cane and looked to be trapped by the traffic flow. I watched the situation for several minutes, and then the old Boy Scout in me sprang into action. I held up my hand to stop the traffic and raced to where the old man was standing.

"Looks like you could use some help," I said.

"What gives you that idea?" he asked sharply.

"Well, you've been standing here for quite a while and haven't made a move."

"Have you considered I might be happy just standing here? Or maybe I'm contemplating suicide but haven't made up my mind?"

"Afraid not. Are you really happy here, or are you thinking of ending it all?"

"Nah, I'm just messing with you. I've been trying to cross this goddamn street for a long time, but the traffic gets worse the longer I stand here."

"How long have you been standing here?" I asked.

"I think this all began last Tuesday or Wednesday."

"You have a cute sense of humor, old man, but I still think you need help. And by the way, have you considered taking along a friend when you go out for a walk?"

"All my friends are dead," he answered. "I just turned ninety-four."

Sorry about the friends," I said. "C'mon, time to cross the street.

I held up my hand again, which caused screeching brakes, a few profanities, and a middle finger or two from irritated drivers. I held his arm as we waded into the street and began a slow shuffle to the far curb.

"It would help if you could move a bit faster," I suggested.

"For me, at this point in my life," he answered, "this is warp speed."

When we reached the other side the old man thanked me, invited me to join him for lunch, and that was the start of a rich and satisfying relationship. The moral of the story is simply this: Sometimes being friendly results in a valuable new friend. Try it—you'll see.

Drinking

"So, what'll you have?"

Walk into any bar, saloon, tavern, or pub and that's the first question you'll hear. Your choice will be absolutely mind-blowing, as experienced bartenders can create a hundred or more different drinks from memory. And if that's not enough, they have recipe books that include about 1000 more concoctions. So "name your poison", as they say. Will it be one of the top ten most popular, such as a Martini, Manhattan, or Margarita? Or does your taste run to the more esoteric, like Rusty Nail, Missionary's Downfall, or perhaps a Pink Squirrel? If you're not the cocktail type there are several hundred kinds of beer, not to mention literally thousands of wines.

Life was not always as rich and varied for those in need of a pick-me-up. Though you may find this hard to believe, alcoholic drinks have been around for at least 10,000 years! You heard right; no matter what you call it, liquor, spirits, booze, firewater, hooch, or rotgut, it all dates back to the Stone Age! Discovery of residue from ancient jugs suggests that intentionally fermented drinks first appeared during the late Neolithic Period. Can you even imagine a caveman, dressed in ill-fitting animal skins, standing there holding a club in one hand while the other clutches a martini? Well, not actually a martini, but a jug of some alcoholic beverage that provided sufficient pleasure in the brain to help early humans survive their primitive existence.

Throughout most of history alcoholic beverages have been used to provide unending enrichment to the social fabric of life. The hardy grain we call barley was first cultivated at about the same time humans abandoned the hunter-gatherer lifestyle and settled down to a more stable life of agriculture and domesticated animals. Barley served as the basic ingredient for bread and beer, both of which formed the chief diet of early tribes. Evidence of barley beer from more than 5000 years ago has been found in Iran, Turkey, and Egypt.

Ancient Egyptians realized–as manual laborers these days will confirm–that after a long day of hard work there is nothing more welcome then a mug of beer. Thus, the thousands of workers who built the Great Pyramids were paid in a daily allotment of bread and beer. One of the first alcoholic beverages to gain popularity in ancient Greece was mead, a fermented drink made from honey and water. Ancient Romans preferred wine diluted with water, as it was not in their culture to drink anything with alcohol at full strength. Alcoholic drinks were first recorded in Europe in the 12th century; and by the early 14th century some form of booze was widely available throughout the continent. During the 16th century alcohol became popular, not only to drink, but also for medicinal purposes. And so it went throughout the world, where in every bar in every neighborhood in every country alcoholic beverages were prized for reducing stress, easing pain, and often making people seem more bold and beautiful than they actually were.

All beers, wines, and spirits contain ethanol, a depressant, which in low doses causes euphoria, relaxation, and sociability; and in higher doses may cause intoxication, stupor, and even unconsciousness. It takes about five minutes for the effect of alcohol to be felt. Once absorbed into the bloodstream it travels from the stomach to the brain and also to the liver. When alcohol in the blood exceeds a certain level, the respiratory system slows down markedly, possibly causing unconsciousness or even a coma. That's not meant to frighten you, unless, of course, you have an unmanageable drinking problem.

Moderate drinking typically produces an overall improvement in mood, possible exhilaration, and increased self-confidence and sociability. Some may also become far more amusing than anyone would dare to predict. So don't be surprised if that boring guy across the room, the one lapping up those Margaritas, soon becomes the life of the party. If you drink a bit too much you may become lethargic, vision may distort, and your speech begins to slur. Drinking beyond that point may result in staggering, walking into a wall, and perhaps throwing up your dinner. Or as Dorothy Parker once claimed, *"After three martinis I'm under the table, and after four I'm under the host."*

It should be obvious to all thinking humans that drinking and driving is a dangerous mix. Alcohol distorts a person's perception and judgment, and those under the influence readily admit their reaction time is slower than when sober. They take chances they would never ordinarily take, and often those chances are fatal. The National Highway Traffic Safety Administration reported that in 2015, more than 10,000 people died in alcohol-related crashes. That accounted for about a third of all highway deaths on U.S. roads, including innocent drivers struck by some drunk's out-of-control vehicle.

Motor vehicle accidents are also the leading cause of death among American teenagers, responsible in fact, for more than one in three deaths of that group. The death of a drunk driver is more than ten times more likely than that of a sober driver. So make your choice before the next beer–drink or drive, you'd be crazy to do both.

Years ago I drove home from my brother's wedding celebration while genuinely plastered. After almost hitting a pedestrian in a crosswalk, I became so frightened I continued home at about ten miles an hour. Since then I have totally avoided "driving under the influence", as the following true story illustrates.

Coming off a freeway ramp late one night I was adjusting my radio, not paying attention, and consequently made a wide turn off the exit ramp. Within an instant I saw the flashing red lights of a police car in my rearview mirror.

"That was a pretty wide turn," the officer said. "You almost crossed into the opposite lane. Have you been drinking?"

Just a glass of wine with dinner," I answered, "But that was hours ago."

He then asked me to step out of the car and walk a straight line. Although the road sloped it two directions I did an acceptable job. He then asked if I could recite the alphabet backwards.

"Probably not," I said. "Can you?"

"Don't get funny with me." he warned.

"Look officer," I said, "I admit I made a bad turn, but it had nothing to do with drinking. I was adjusting my radio and looked away for an instant. Really, I'm sober." There was a long pause before I added, "You know, there may be a neighborhood bank being robbed right now, or some junkie is beating up his girlfriend, or someone, somewhere might really need your help. And since I'm five minutes from home and basically a peace-loving, sober guy, what say you give me a ticket for a lousy turn, and let's call it a night?"

The officer stood quietly for a long moment and then said, "Just be more careful next time." Then he put away his book, turned, and walked back to his patrol car.

According to the 2015 National Survey on Drug Use and Health, eighty-six percent of people ages 18 or older reported that they drank alcohol at some point in their lifetime, All that drinking adds up to a fifty-billion-dollar industry supported annually by American drinkers.

Ever since the discovery and delight of mild intoxication, there have been forces of righteousness determined to put an end to all that pleasure. Prior to the Civil War, a wave of religious revivalism swept the country, leading to increased calls for abstinence; and by the turn of the century, temperance societies were a common fixture across the country. Alcohol was seen as a destructive force in families and marriages, while saloon culture was viewed as corrupt and ungodly. In 1919, Congress ratified the 18th Amendment, which banned the manufacture, transportation, and sale of intoxicating liquors. Prohibition had begun.

Despite an immediate decline in arrests for drunkenness and a thirty percent drop in alcohol consumption, those who wanted to continue drinking found ever-more inventive ways to do so. The illegal bootlegging of liquor went on throughout the decade, along with the operation of speakeasies, the smuggling of alcohol across state lines, and the illegal production of moonshine or bathtub gin in private homes.

There were a few interesting exceptions to the ban on alcohol distribution. Sacramental wine was permitted for religious purposes, leading to a sudden increase in the number of new priests and rabbis.

Also, drug stores were allowed to sell "medicinal whiskey" to treat every condition from toothaches to the flu. With a physician's prescription, "patients" could legally buy a pint of hard liquor every ten days. Pharmaceutical liquor often came with nonsensical medical orders such as *"Take three ounces every hour for stimulant—until stimulated."*

Many speakeasies operated under the guise of being pharmacies, and legitimate establishments flourished. For example, Walgreens, the huge drugstore chain grew from around twenty locations to more than five hundred during the 1920s. Prohibition also encouraged the rise of criminal activity and gang violence, such as that perpetrated by Al Capone and others who profited enormously dealing in illegal liquor.

By 1932 the country was mired in the Great Depression, and the idea of creating jobs and revenue by once again legalizing the liquor industry had an undeniable appeal. Democratic candidate, Franklin D. Roosevelt, easily won the election over Herbert Hoover, and quickly proposed an amendment repealing Prohibition. It was reported that FDR celebrated his legislative success by enjoying his preferred drink—a dirty martini.

Alcoholic beverages have always had supporters as well as detractors. Its most credible claim is that moderate drinking has beneficial effects on health, especially among older people, including decreased risks for heart disease, stroke, and diabetes. Alcoholic drinks are also a source of food energy, as well as carbohydrates. For example, beer contains sufficient amounts to increase body weight, leading to the ever prominent "beer belly". Your health may not be the reason to begin hitting the bottle, but it may serve as an excuse to mix up a batch of martinis. You might claim, "I get little pleasure from this, but my doctor insists it's good for my heart."

And speaking of martinis, my drink of choice for many years, I remain particularly annoyed when I hear the term "vodka martini". Vodka was a relatively new spirit that appeared in the U.S. shortly after World War II. As bartenders were unsure how to use it, they began by copying gin-based recipes and soon came up with a vodka and vermouth concoction called the "Kangaroo". As it strongly resembled the popular gin martini, patrons began to request, "that martini drink made with vodka". Soon thereafter, the Kangaroo tag was abandoned. Nevertheless, I feel obliged to set the story straight. A martini is made with gin! A copycat drink using vodka may or may not be a Kangaroo, but I can assure you, it absolutely will never, ever be a martini.

There are many reasons to avoid liquor—excessive consumption being the leading one. An estimated 90,000 die each year from alcohol-related causes, making alcohol the fourth leading preventable cause of death in the United States. In recent years, binge drinking alone cost the country about $200 billion. So, to all you pie-eyed drinkers out there, never forget that old adage: Everything in moderation. Everything!

W.C. Fields, famous actor, writer, comedian, and hard-drinking misanthrope once said, *"I often cook with wine. Sometimes I even add it to the food."* So cooking with liquor does not literally mean you should flip hamburgers on the grill with one hand while holding a cold beer in the other hand. It means that using alcohol to enhance certain dishes is a classic and valuable technique of fine cooking. Where would *Coq au Vin* be without the *Vin*? And Cherries Jubilee wouldn't be much of a celebration without the excitement of flaming brandy, or would Beef Bourguignon be anything but a flavorless stew without a generous quantity of rich red wine.

When used appropriately, alcohol improves food by bonding with fat and water molecules, allowing it to enhance aromas and flavor. In a marinade, alcohol helps to season the meat, while in cooked sauces it makes food smell and taste better. One should use the same alcohol you would drink—nothing undrinkable and no "cooking wine," which is an inexpensive beverage not fit for consumption, unless you're truly broke and desperate.

So whether you're flavoring meat or seafood, or even poaching fruit, like pears in wine, try a little liquor. It won't make you drunk, but it might make your guests giddy enough to conclude you've a lot more talent than someone who can barely scramble an egg.

Finally, there is the question, why do people drink? There are many answers to that question, sadly, many of them excuses for overdoing. Some drink to alleviate the stress of everyday life; others drink to lose their inhibitions and become socially more charming. Ernest Hemingway said, *"I drink to make other people more interesting,"*

A certain percentage of people drink to get drunk, and they are generally aware of what they are doing until they do something regrettable. At that point they often give up alcohol entirely, until perhaps the next time. W.C. Fields said, *"Swearing off drinking is easy, I've done it thousands of times." Even* Robert Benchley, the humorist said, *"I know I'm drinking myself into a slow death, but then, I'm in no hurry.*

The last word on drinking belongs to the many who have said, *"I only drink on two occasions, when I'm thirsty and when I'm not."*

So here's looking at you, kid, whoever you are. Bottoms up and down the hatch!

Sex

All of life revolves around sex. That isn't just my opinion–though I heartily agree–it's an essential principle developed by Sigmund Freud during the last century. According to Freud, there are only two basic drives that motivate all thoughts, emotions, and behavior: sex and aggression. Those drives underlie every impulse of human experience. While some believe Freud's stress on sex was exaggerated, most consider his views to be one of the most significant contributions ever made to the understanding of sexuality.

Sexual activity among all animal life leads to procreation–to bringing about new life–which assures survival of the species. Aggression, on the other hand, is a way to protect us from those threatening to do us harm. It allows us to procreate, while at the same time stop those who may try to prevent us from doing so.

As to the proposition of life revolving around sex, the Bible tells us that Adam and Eve were created as an object of God's love. They were made to be loved by God and to bring Him pleasure. It could be argued, however, that it was Adam and Eve who derived the greater pleasure. There they were, rent-free in the Garden of Eden, plenty of food, no clothes, and the dictate from God to "Go forth and multiply". Furthermore, they knew no guilt or shame until that ill-fated episode involving the serpent and apple business. Some religious authorities claim there was no sexual passion between the first couple until they were banished from Eden. If that's true, then why was it called Paradise? And since no one else was there to observe, who really knows what sort of hanky-panky went on?

That's Life

From the beginning of civilization people realized that sex was so incredibly pleasurable, that overdoing it would leave little time for anything else. Thus, restrictions were developed to control the free and easy ways of primitive life. The return of Moses from Mount Sinai with God's Ten Commandments acknowledged that people were pretty much running amok and in need of strict rules to live by, not only for sex, but for antisocial activities like lying, stealing, and murder, all of which degraded a respectable society. Two of the Commandments recognized the prevalence of disruptive sex: Adultery and Coveting, especially coveting your neighbor's wife, which of course, was simply more Adultery.

Somewhat later, the church got into the act by developing prohibitions further frustrating those seeking a guilt-free sex life. Every major religion developed moral codes covering issues of sexuality and ethics that sought to influence and regulate people's most personal practices. The Christian sexual ethic, for example, was developed two thousand years ago and, amazingly, is still endorsed by some churches today. It stated that there was exactly one way for Christians to express their sexuality, and that was by remaining abstinent until they were married to a person of the opposite gender. Even within marriage, sex was tolerated for reproductive purposes, but couples were not particularly encouraged to *enjoy* the act. You can just imagine an early Christian in that situation perhaps claiming, "I'm really not getting much pleasure in this, but… Oh God! Oh God! Oh God!

St. Paul, the celibate Christian leader who wrote much of the New Testament, thought that practicing celibacy would bring you closer to God, since it would allow you to concentrate on spiritual, rather than physical matters. He said nothing, however, about handling the increased frustration or the surreptitious abuse of choirboys that followed.

After Early Christians produced several children they were expected to stop having sex altogether. St. Augustine, from about the year 400, promoted the notion that sexual desire, or lust, was a sin; as was premarital sex or having sex simply for pleasure. St. Augustine was known as a respected theologian and philosopher, but he was hardly what you'd consider today "a fun-loving guy".

During the Middle Ages the church became even more intrusive; while virginity and monogamy were prized, homosexuality was often punished by death. Really, death! The church became specific on the permissible type of sex married couples could have. Since all sex was strictly for procreation, certain positions were banned; for example, no sex standing up. It's difficult to imagine anyone being seriously inconvenienced by that restriction, other than perhaps acrobatic circus performers. Even when couples were prone there was insistence on the "missionary position", that is, the women *always* on the bottom. Strictly banned were doggy style, oral and anal sex, and of course, masturbation. One wonders how church officials even knew what those activities were. Do you suppose they learned of them first hand? Oh, perish that blasphemous thought!

There were also restrictions on when people could have sex: Never on fast days, or feast days for a saint, or on Sundays, for example. All of these prohibitions meant that on average, sex between married couples was permissible perhaps once a week—if that. Many, of course, ignored the church and chose to do whatever they pleased, pretty much as they still do today. If, as a result, they had a rollicking good time, they generally faced a lifetime of guilt.

These days, according to the Public Religion Research Institute, almost all American couples have sex before marriage, including eighty percent of people identified as born-again Christians, evangelicals, and fundamentalists. They also feel it morally acceptable to use contraception. Nevertheless, most religions still continue to define proper standards of sexual conduct, most of which have a negative connotation. For example, "sex before marriage is wicked" and "sex for mere pleasure is immoral". As a result, when you get married you are supposed to immediately shed years of guilt and fear about sex and have a great time. Sadly, that happens about as often as you purchase a winning lottery ticket.

Wilhelm Reich, the Austrian psychoanalyst, concluded years ago that, *"Sexual suppression supports the power of the Church, exploiting the masses by sexual anxiety and guilt."* Reich was a sexual evangelist who held that satisfactory orgasm made the difference between sickness and health. He believed sex was the panacea for all ills and eventually concluded that the only thing wrong with neurotic patients was, "the lack of full and repeated sexual satisfaction". So listen to Wilhelm, folks, do what comes naturally, and have a healthy and guilt-free good time.

As though morality needed another constraint, the Hays Code for motion pictures was adopted and began enforcement in 1934. The Code was a strict set of rules governing American cinema for over three decades. During the early Hollywood years there were numerous public complaints about the perceived lewd content of films, and the ensuing media frenzy resulted in the call for government action. Offending examples included remarks from actress and writer Mae West, such as, *"Is that a gun in your pocket, or are you just happy to see me?"* As well as, *"When I'm good I'm very good, but when I'm bad I'm better."*

To stop the government from censoring or banning films, Hollywood decided to discipline itself with the Hays Code; a set of production directives created mostly by the clergy and voluntarily adopted by all major studios. Not all Hays Code restrictions were leveled against sexual content, but following are a few that were:

- *Nudity and references to sexual behavior are prohibited.*
- *Perverse topics such as homosexuality, miscegenation, bestiality, and venereal diseases may not be discussed or depicted in any way.*
- *Sleeping Single (twin beds) shall be universal, even for married couples.*
- *In all romantic scenes a woman must have at least one foot on the floor.*
- *The sanctity of marriage must be upheld.*

Other Hays Code directives included depicting religion in a respectful manner, avoiding excessive drug or liquor consumption, blasphemy, and profanity. Clark Gable's famous line in "Gone with the Wind": *"Frankly my dear, I don't give a damn."* was only permitted because mild swearing was in the original novel. In 1948, the Supreme

Court restricted the ability to enforce the Hays Code over all films shown in the U.S., and by 1966, a new Film Rating System ultimately replaced the Code.

Casual sex these days seems to be more pervasive than ever before. Movies, television shows, and popular songs are so abundant with examples of uncommitted sex that many critics suggest that hooking up is replacing traditional dating as the primary means of developing relationships among young people. Data from the General Social Survey reveals that there is indeed more casual sex and less romantic sex than in previous generations, but dating is nowhere near obsolete. Further research shows that the most frequent casual partner is more a "friend-with-benefit" situation than sex with a random stranger. That's another good reason, if you needed one, to become a friendlier person.

Among the Ten Commandments regularly ignored, I would guess that Adultery and Lying about it is the double-barreled winner. Depending on studies, it has been estimated that up to 50% of men and 30 % of women had sex with someone other than their spouse at least once during their marriage. That statistic means that if you are not currently cheating on your spouse, it's a safe bet the guy next door probably is.

Many cultures have considered adultery a serious crime, often incurring severe punishment—usually for the woman, but sometimes for the man—including mutilation, torture, or occasionally, execution. Such punishments have gradually fallen into disfavor everywhere, and adultery in the U.S. is no longer considered a criminal offense.

The causes of infidelity are numerous. The recurrent clichés are a need for sex and adventure. But in many cases what is truly lacking can be something else entirely, for example, a desire for change. Perhaps, after several years of marriage, the thrill is gone; the spouse has changed, and the routine of a boring life creates a need for shaking up the status quo.

Some seek reassurance, a feeling of being loved and understood again. Some may wonder if they're still appealing enough to seduce a new partner, while others want to experience the excitement of falling in love all over again. In other words, no one emotion applies to every situation. Whether it's the diminished frequency of sexual relations, ego gratification, or simply the adventure of new and exciting sex, adultery remains a popular solution.

Sadly, infidelity often creates more problems than it solves. Temptation is everywhere and resistance is difficult, but if your marriage is truly beyond salvation, experts suggest you take the honorable path, join the ranks of the unmarried first, and then go crazy with the new sexual partner of your erotic fantasies.

They say that sex sells. The effectiveness of sensual advertising continues to be debated, but ad experts claim that when used skillfully, sex is one of the strongest and most effective sales tools. There is nothing new about sexy advertising; the earliest examples go back to the late 1800s with scantily clad models advertising tobacco and liquor. Clairol hair dye launched its famous campaign in the 1970s with beautiful models and the suggestive slogan: *"Does she… or doesn't she? Only her hairdresser knows for sure."* Then there was the Calvin Klein ad featuring 16-year-old Brooke Shields in jeans with the caption *"Want to know what gets between me and my Calvin's? Nothing."*

Because we are so strongly wired to sex many respond to erotic imagery even when subtly presented; like the photo of a sleek convertible with the slogan, *"Topless"*. And when it comes to models, an ankle or nape of neck can be nearly as effective as showing an entire figure. Not every product is easily linked to erotic suggestion, but certain products are a natural, Victoria's Secret, for example, employs some of the most glorious semi-nudes on earth to promote their products. In fact any company selling lingerie would be foolish to show anything other than beautiful bodies.

Some products may stretch a bit to employ sexy models. Carl's Jr. for example, has often shown gorgeous models virtually making love to a hamburger, complete with special sauce running down the chin. Is the sandwich that good? Who cares? Automobile advertising has been associated with sex for many years. It is one of the products easily linked to erotic messages. Car companies want their products to be perceived as sexy, fast, and daring, so even the image of a speeding car racing into a tunnel projects a picture-perfect sexual expression.

Sex

Someone once said that, "Sex is like air, not very important until you're deprived of it". The act itself may be universal, but people's experiences and attitudes are not. Some worry that what they're experiencing is abnormal, or could they be doing something wrong? Relax; when it comes to sex, there is no such thing as "normal". Whatever two people agree to do is normal for them, because there's no wrong way to experience sex.

Some believe that an advanced degree in sexology is required to fully appreciate sexual relations. Nothing could be further from the truth. If, for example, you are bewildered about the location of every erogenous zone, remember this: Women have multiple zones that provide great satisfaction, while men realize similar gratification from their one all-purpose zone that may extend from the eyebrows to the toes.

Two different people may have different sex drives, so sex once a week might be either overdoing it or insufficient. If you feel there is something wrong, perhaps it's time to talk things over with your partner. It is important to remember that, thrilling or not, sexual relations provides intimacy, while promoting emotional and physical health. In other words, it's good for you.

My doctor once said, *"Sex is like pizza; even when it's mediocre it's wonderful."* Over the years, many others have added their opinions for this most universal of all activities.

- Author, John Updike declared, *"Sex is like money; only too much is enough."*
- Woody Allen stated, *"I don't know the question, but sex is definitely the answer."*
- Billy Crystal said, *"Women need a reason to have sex, men just need a place."*

Other anonymous contributors were responsible for the following one-liners:

That's Life

- *Love thy neighbor—but don't get caught.*
- *Sex is only dirty if done correctly.*
- *Sex on an elevator is wrong on so many levels.*

As the above convincingly prove, in addition to it's other considerable benefits, sex can also be the source of a few good laughs.

Death

If you are uncomfortable thinking about death, it's perfectly okay to stop reading now, because there's not much positive to say about dying. As far as I'm concerned, nothing is more completely final than death. No more kisses, no more rainbows, and no more hot fudge sundaes, just to mention a few things worth living for. Of course those suffering constant pain might prefer to be dead, but for others, holding the grim reaper at arm's length seems a no-brainer.

Dying is the inevitable end of life. No one escapes it, but we are biologically programmed to resist it. You should understand that every day after your birth you're heading downhill towards that ultimate finish line. We all have a limited time on earth, and then, ready or not, the party is over. Most people have no idea when that time will be, and that's a good thing; but we all hope it will be long into the future. An unfortunate few die before their time in nasty and horrible ways, like a car crash, drug overdose, or drive-by shooting. But most die of old age—the truly fortunate, while asleep in their beds.

Almost everyone fears death, but many say it's not actually being dead that bothers them; rather it's the process of dying and possibly the pain they might suffer. Most agree with Woody Allen, who once said, *"I'm not afraid of death; I just don't want to be there when it happens."* Others say their greatest fear is the unknown, not being certain if there's an afterlife or possibly facing nothingness forever. Some worry about how loved ones will continue without them, or about their unfinished projects, while a few regret missing that long planned trip to Machu Picchu. In other words, it's like being fatally struck by lightning just before revealing the punch line of a really funny joke. You're never going to hear the laughter, or even be able to explain it to the guy who doesn't "get" it. Sad to say, there's rarely a convenient time to die.

People have been concerned about the afterlife for centuries. More than 5000 years ago a major influence on the lives of ancient Egyptians was the religious belief of life after death. The concept of an everlasting life pervaded all manners and customs. To achieve immortality of the soul it was essential to preserve in death all that had existed in life. Thus, bodies were embalmed and mummified, and tombs were filled with every possession of the deceased, including furniture, utensils, and jewelry. Thus, the tomb became an artistic storehouse that provided everything in death the deceased had known during life. Excavated tombs, therefore, allow us today to know much about how ancient Egyptians once lived.

Somewhat later in history, Christians believed the promise by Jesus that one's soul would have an everlasting life. Others were not so certain. First of all, we should understand the meaning of "soul". It is defined as the spiritual part of humans, as distinct from the physical part; in other words, soul is the disembodied spirit of a deceased person. Humans are made up of complex chemical reactions. Those who believe in an afterlife accept the idea that when we die the chemical reactions stop, but they claim, the soul continues to exist.

Nonbelievers, on the other hand, say the entire notion of "soul" is a complete myth. The concept was invented by religions because so many people were distressed facing their own mortality. Some may feel better knowing that a part of them will go on, but the concept of "soul", they claim, is a total fabrication. Skeptics further declare you can throw angels, halos, and harps into that same basket of bogus baloney.

Belief in an afterlife has been compared to the notion of Santa Claus. Reindeer cannot fly any more than an overweight man can slide down a chimney. Also, how can a single sleigh carry all the toys for all the kids in the world? It's obvious that Santa is a clever invention, very much like your "soul". The fact is, when chemical reactions stop, so do you. Sorry to pop that bubble, but logic says death is truly the end of the line.

Death

Advocates of an afterlife claim that its main advantage is reuniting with, let's say, Aunt Josephine and Uncle Walter. With apologies for throwing a wet blanket over that notion, consider this: It is estimated that in the history of the world about 100 billion people have died. Let's assume about 20 percent were so evil they went directly to hell. Figure another 10 percent are in purgatory, not good enough for heaven, but not quite evil enough for hell. That leaves about 70 billion people now residing in heaven. So tell me, how do you plan to find Aunt Josephine and Uncle Walter? Is there a heavenly directory? My guess is that you probably have the same chance of running into Cleopatra or Charlie Chaplin. Reuniting with dead relatives may sound appealing, but there's always the risk you'll bump into the in-laws who didn't particularly like you when you were all alive. You might actually have better luck trying a séance.

Reincarnation is another form of afterlife in which the soul, upon death of the body, comes back to earth in another body or form. To realize that you've lived many lives before this one, with many more to come, is attractive and comforting. You may consider the problems and predicaments of this life relatively unimportant, since having another life offers a chance to start over and get it right. Nearly a billion Hindus and a half-billion Buddhists, not to mention ancient Greeks, certain Jews and a few Christians, have believed for thousands of years in reincarnation. Some 25 percent of Americans today also believe that you're born, you die, and your soul is born again in another human, or perhaps in the family's pet goldfish. Similar to the concept of "soul", the religious invention of "reincarnation" has its adherents as well as detractors. If you believe in the concept, by all means go for it. But don't be surprised if you come back as a dancing cockatoo, rather than a beauty queen.

Suicide is the act of intentionally causing your own death. The reason one commits suicide includes depression, stress, and a seriously troubled life. There were more than 40,000 suicides in the U.S in 2014, according to the Center for Disease Control, making it the tenth leading cause of death overall.

Since we are all born with a survival instinct, it's difficult to fathom how a person can ignore that instinct, disregard the wonders of life, and abandon every possibility of future happiness. How can a person casually jump off the Golden Gate Bridge or pull the trigger of a gun to the head. In the mind of someone contemplating suicide, the act is a way to eliminate pain—the kind of pain most of us will never know. The thought of suicide occurs when a person feels they've run out of solutions to problems that seem intolerable and unrelenting. Most believe that suicide doesn't really solve anything, but a suicidal person feels that putting an end to life is their last, best, and *only* solution.

The goal of a suicide bomber is a bit different. True, the bomber commits suicide, but the objective is to destroy an enemy, rather than eliminate personal pain. Suicide bombing is a weapon that requires willing individuals, an organization to train and use them, and a society that promotes that act in the name of a greater good. The term "martyr" has been applied to bombers, because they sacrifice their lives on behalf of a nobler cause, such as religion or a societal obligation. Thus, the implied heroism and reverence tends to make it more attractive to recruits.

Suicide bombing began years ago when combatants died while attempting to get close enough to their targets to be more effective. Toward the end of World War II the desperate Japanese Kamikaze were literally flying bombs piloted by suicidal humans against American naval forces. Their purpose was to cause maximum destruction, while sending a message of fanaticism and intimidation. Suicide bombers became prevalent in the Middle East during the 1980s, and now there is almost no place on earth safe from indiscriminate and devastating suicidal attacks.

A personal curiosity is the promise made to potential suicide bombers of seventy-two virgins eagerly awaiting them in paradise. Why seventy-two, you may ask? An Islamic scripture states, *"Allah Most High shall provide every man with six dozen wives in heaven. Wide-eyed, her attraction never lags, nor shall his arousal ever wane."*

On the face of it, it sounds like a wonderfully wild sexual adventure, but upon further thought, I foresee trouble ahead. First, where will they all live? Even with a pair of double-decker bunks in every room you would need eighteen bedrooms plus an endless number of bathrooms. Next, how can anyone remember the names of seventy-two sexual partners? Even Hugh Hefner would have had a problem. I suppose you could just assign numbers. But what if #56 tries to sneak ahead of #48, who's to keep the whole process orderly? Finally, if the former suicide bomber sleeps with one virgin each night he would need about two-and-a-half months to complete a round trip of his harem. On the other hand, if he shtups two virgins each night, or has an occasional threesome, he could cut the time in half.

There is also the critical question of why a suicide bomber would prefer a single virgin in the first place, not to mention seventy-two of them? If he knew anything at all about sex he would know that when the action begins the virgin might very well continue to lie there like a dead herring. And if he suggests she might show a little enthusiasm, she might say, "This is all so new to me. You have to remember, I'm a virgin." The dead suicide bomber may now think, "With seventy-one more of these rookie nookies waiting in the wings, why in the name of Allah did I bother to blow myself up?"

An obituary is a news article that reports the recent death of a person, typically along with age, an account of the person's life, and information about the upcoming funeral or memorial service. Skilled writers, who highlight the accomplishments and salient features of one's life, compose the most professional of these. Others appear to be written by friends or relatives whose goal is to convince St Peter, as well as the rest of the world, that this guy (or gal) should get a free pass for a box seat in Paradise. Those who might be grasping for ideas might write, as one desperate person did, "He is survived by 547 Facebook followers."

Nothing negative appears in most obituaries, as one chooses to remember only the goodness of the dearly departed, even though he may have lacked a single crumb of common decency. There have been individuals who cheated on spouses, left a string of unpaid bills, and never, ever, gave a cent to charity; yet the obituary invariably begins, "Spencer Schmidlap, beloved husband, devoted father, and trusted friend, passed away..." That's another peculiarity—people rarely die, they pass away, or simply pass; as if when you look out the window you might catch a glimpse of them going by.

There is something about death that many find funny, perhaps because it's so frightening. Woody Allen has obsessed about the subject for years, as in those that follow:

- *I do not believe in an afterlife, although I am bringing a change of underwear.*
- *It is impossible to experience one's death objectively and still carry a tune.*
- *Death should not be seen as the end, but as an effective way to cut down expenses.*

Another couple of jokes that may take the sting out of death:

A Rabbi asks if anyone would like to add a good word about the deceased. Not a single hand goes up. "Please," says the Rabbi, "anyone—say something." At long last an old man slowly rises and says, "His brother was worse."

Finally, *a man is asked what he would like to hear friends say as they pass his open casket. "It would be nice," he answers, "if someone would say, 'I think I just saw him move!'"*

Since we're all going to die at some point, you can make things a lot easier on your survivors if you get everything in order before that unhappy moment. This will ensure that others understand what you want to happen after you're gone. Everyone should have a last will and testament designating what happens with your property and naming an executor who carries out your wishes after you die. At the very least, having a will should discourage vultures from descending on your estate and carting off, for example, your stamp collection or great-grandfather's Civil War musket. Sadly, half of all Americans have no will.

It's probably sensible to consider appointing a trusted person as your power of attorney in the event you become incapacitated. A power of attorney allows the person to handle financial or legal matters, if you fall ill or are unable to handle them for yourself. Otherwise you may spend your final years drugged and unhappy in some "rest" home where you're mostly ignored, the food is terrible, and nobody cares. A good representative may even see to it that meals improve.

Next, you should indicate if you want to be buried, cremated, or frozen for eternity. As many may realize, when you're dead, you're dead, so who really cares? The same applies to a memorial service; if you have a preference, leave explicit instructions. Otherwise, your family might decide that the finest tribute they can pay you is using your life insurance proceeds for a week or two in Paris.

Getting your affairs in order is very much like taking out the garbage; nobody is thrilled to have that responsibility, but everybody feels better once it happens. So get up right now and do your part–it's time to be a *mensch* and take out the garbage.

One final word of advice: It is my firm belief that we should all live our lives in the most exemplary way possible, so at the very end, when speakers at our memorial services say that "he or she will be missed", those words will not sound trite or hollow, but rather will be sincere and come straight from the heart.